STEVEN HELLER

GRAPHIC STYLE LAB

ROCKPAPERINK

branding • typography • logos • color • design
management • design for change • posters • fashion
www.RockPaperInk.com

First published in the United States of America in 2015 by
Rockport Publishers, a member of
Quarto Publishing Group USA Inc.
100 Cummings Center
Suite 406-L
Beverly, Massachusetts 01915-6101
Telephone: (978) 282-9590
Fax: (978) 283-2742
www.rockpub.com
Visit RockPaperInk.com to share your opinions, creations, and passion for design.

10 9 8 7 6 5 4 3 2 1

ISBN: 978-1-59253-910-9

Digital edition published in 2015
eISBN: 978-1-62788-056-5

Library of Congress Cataloging-in-Publication Data available

Design: Rick Landers
Cover Image: Rick Landers

Printed in China

ABOUT THE AUTHOR

Steven Heller is the cochair and cofounder of SVA MFA Design/Designer as Author + Entrepreneur. He is the author of 170 books on design and visual culture. In 1999, he received the AIGA Lifetime Achievement Medal, and in 2011 he earned the Smithsonian's National Design Award for "Design Mind."

CONTENTS

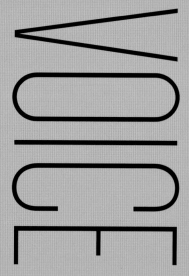

NO. 4
....

PLAYING WITH

ATTITUDE

NO. 5
....

PLAYING WITH

SIMPLICITY + COMPLEXITY

NO. 6
....

PLAYING WITH
Symbolic

TYPE

–GRAPHIC–
STYLE

–GRAPHIC–
STYLE

–GRAPHIC–
STYLE

–GRAPHIC–
STYLE

–GRAPHIC–
STYLE

–GRAPHIC–
STYLE

–GRAPHIC–
STYLE

STEVEN HELLER

PERSONAL STYLE:
PRO AND CON

"Should I have a personal style? What is style?

Is it right to borrow styles?"

These are the most common questions from design and illustration students—and rightly so. Style is a precarious notion.

Often style is considered more important than substance. Sometimes style is substance. This book attempts to answer these questions through fifty exercises/case studies of how styles are used (sometimes abused) and how they can evolve into a distinct design personality, if only temporarily, for the designer. The case studies address the distinctions between personal and universal style, historical and contemporary style, one-of-a kind styles, and how lettering, type, and typography can define style.

Everyone has personal characteristics that distinguish or identify one from another. That is style. All designers use stylistic elements in their work. Style is an essential marker. So choosing a style or styles is critical. Sometimes the content of an assignment demands a certain style. Sometimes a designer simply wants to have a certain look. Whatever the rationale, it is important to know the options. This book is about how to experiment, or play, with styles to become more adept inside and outside of the classroom. Through fifty examples of professional and student work, *Graphic Style Lab* will provide the impetus for designers—beginning and practicing—to learn more about the role style plays in the theater of design.

HAVE FUN...

Play triggers a creative chain reaction that results in graphic design. Without play, design is an orchestrated symphony of visual and textual components neatly composed for a particular purpose. With play, design is like improvisational jazz, a concert of many signs and symbols. Duke Ellington could have been talking about playing with graphic style when he said about jazz: "You've got to find some way of saying it without saying it." This applies to design and designers, too.

Can there be anything more satisfying, albeit stressful, than sitting in front of an empty screen (or piece of paper, if you prefer) with infinite options at your fingertips for expressing yourself through graphics and typography? I recall my elementary school art class—before all the state funding dried up and everyone was required to take an extra period of Mr. Carnahan's wood shop—when, as a respite from a preset three-Rs curriculum, students were given license to veer blithely into the impromptu realm of creative serendipity. Such freedoms are often discouraged in the real world, and even graphic designers (although we are artists at heart) are reticent, especially when starting out in the profession, to embrace the infinite options of creative outreach known as play.

Some design pundits argue, however, that graphic design is not about license but rather about establishing order and structure from chaos. When chaos is the enemy, simplicity and cleanliness are the ultimate virtues. Some classic graphic designs that conform strictly to formalistic dogma are indeed admired and revered for flawless precision. And why not? Precision is a good thing—in moderation.

A significant proportion of exceptional designs have also busted those same admirably rigid dictates. Just as chaos breeds order, order breeds the need to examine less orthodox alternatives, which invariably requires play.

Play is abandon born of exploration; play activates that sense of uncertainty about what lies around the corner, yet you go there anyway. While following a strict design template may, for specific jobs such as an IRS form, be the right course of action, nothing beats play for creative profit. Play is neither following nor leading but rather remaining open to and engaging with unanticipated possibilities, free from the doctrinaire formalism that can erode creative instincts.

There are plenty of psycho-sociological theories that describe the mental health benefits of play as, for instance, a therapeutic release of tension or a pathway to enhanced cognition. These theories have names such as *complexity theory*, *play learning*, *knowledge structures*, *theory of mind*, and more. If you are inclined to learn more about, say, Piagetian and Vygotskian theories or the relationship between play and social, imagination, and literacy development, you should fiddle (e.g., play) around on Google—it's all there. This book, on the other hand, is concerned with how to and what to play with so that you might find your own voice through graphic design and typography.

All designers have opportunities to play in different playgrounds and with many playthings. The more media access there is, the greater the chance of some kind of fruitful play taking place. Yet the more imposed restrictions there are, the better the chance of encountering, challenging, and then busting taboos—although, let's be clear, not all play is rebellious.

Play is active participation in the process of creation while testing the tolerances of the status quo. Play is a means of combining unknown with familiar to create novel. Chemists play when they combine a known substance with an untested one. Musicians literally and figuratively play when they meld disharmonic and contrasting sounds. Graphic designers play when they impulsively change or blend the styles that they are best known for to find other directions. It takes guts to play—seriously!

Designers who frequently change their graphic styles are not just restless or insecure—they are gambling that what's new and challenging for them is within the bounds of what a client finds acceptable. Obviously, needing acceptability runs counter to what has been said so far about the abandon inherent in playing. But the two are not contradictory. In graphic design, playing involves risk: no risk, no play. Changing styles means playing with other voices and personalities—it is often risky.

Style is a marker of a time or place, technique or technology, attitude or sensibility, signature or voice. These are positive attributes, but graphic style can just as readily be a crutch that holds up some very successful designers who rely on familiar conceits and tried-and-true methods to get them through a design problem. It works, too. But for some, even when their style is not derivative—which is rare—a timeworn approach can be taken for granted, ignored, or considered passé.

One of the most irritating phrases a designer can hear from a client is "Make it fresh." A personal style, even if it is borrowed, is so inextricably embedded in a designer's wiring that demanding change can have a disastrous effect. Yet it can also be the new lease on life. The fact is this: Nobody should stand still. Or to paraphrase Woody Allen in Annie Hall, a design career is like a shark. It has to constantly move forward or it dies. So, don't get caught with a dead shark on your hands.

This book does not guarantee a new lease or a temporary sublet on your creative life, but through fifty different exercises you will see how others have achieved their perfect solutions for particular problems. There are thousands of graphic design problems in various media that you will face during your creative lifetime. This book cannot offer solutions for even a small fraction of those. But it will, I hope, encourage you to play with different graphic styles, expressions, impressions, and attitudes. The exercises herein are drawn from two sources: 1. Undergraduate and graduate classes, where the styles or visual languages were open-ended, while the criteria for success was how well it fit the solution. 2. Professional (published or printed), where the styles used were considered for both appropriateness to the solution and for the fun of making the work.

The exercises are not here to be copied as such. Unless you are parodying or satirizing something, do not imitate what you see. That undermines the essence of play, which is an attempt to conceive new creative possibilities from old and novel. Instead, use these exercises as spark plugs for your own engine. How would you design a poster criticizing homophobia (see Miccio, page 62), or the interior for a hip restaurant in Abilene, Texas (see Rogers, page 72), or an ad campaign protesting child sex traffic (see Seetoh, page 60)? Determine which are the most appealing graphic styles and how you might employ them for projects without slavishly following them. Most of all, this book is about play. See how these designers play. See how you might play with them.

HOW TO PLAY:

These exercises are not your typical A + B = C formulae. You are not going to be pulled along by a string of step-by-steps. Each solution in this book is a studio's or individual's response to a specific set of criteria. Your job is to interpret and reinterpret the solutions you see here. So do the following:

1. Read the description.
2. Look closely at the visual material.
3. Determine what you want to learn from the exercise.
4. Restate the problem to fit your goal.
5. Respond to the problem with your own design.

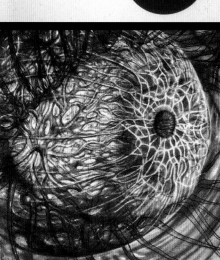

A GLOSSARY

KNOW THE STYLES YOU'RE PLAYING WITH

V intage clothing stores are more than places to buy new/old fashions. They are reliquaries of history. Vintage graphic design, likewise, is more than a swap shop where one style is traded for another. Designers can learn a great deal about art, culture, and technology—context—from the historical styles they experiment or play with. But before trying on or taking a style for a spin, get to know the historical options that are available. Playing with graphic style is more satisfying when there is fluency at the core.

ARTS AND CRAFTS

Founded in England by **William Morris** (1834–1896), arts and crafts was an alternative design movement more or less from 1860 to 1910, with offshoots in the United States (Roycrofters, Stickley, etc.) and elsewhere. It was led by the artist, designer, writer, and social critic William Morris and inspired by the writings of critics **John Ruskin** (1819–1900) and **Augustus Pugin** (1812–1852). With its emphasis on handwork and its revival of Gothic styling, arts and crafts (also known as the aesthetic movement) was philosophically based on a critique against industrialization and the impoverished state of decorative arts in Great Britain. The output of arts and crafts communities was based on traditional craftsmanship often influenced by medieval, romantic, or folk styles of decoration. The movement advocated economic and social reform. Other workshops developed around the world, but none with as much far-reaching and long-respected influence. It is known for its naturalist graphic motifs, a precursor of art nouveau.

ART DECO

Launched in Paris at the 1925 Exposition internationale des arts décoratifs et industriels modernes, l'art moderne (also referred to as modernistic) was a major commercial style designed to supplant the eccentricities of art nouveau. As it happened, it was no less decoratively ostentatious, but in a more "modern" and thus contemporary way. Rather than curvilinear, its signature motifs were rectilinear; instead of excessive amounts of floriated decoration, it was more machine-like in its linearity. The term *art deco* is a contraction of the original exposition coined in the 1970s for one of the exhibitions to show off deco's wares. The style did, however, underscore not only a period but also an attitude that continues to hold sway as a marker of the period when it flourished.

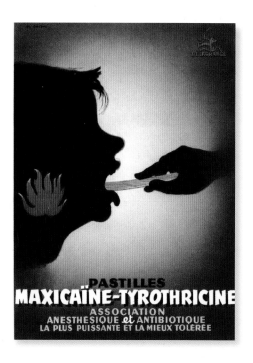

ART NOUVEAU

Launched in Paris in 1896 after the first waves of Japonisme (1870s) hit French shores, art nouveau had many names in various nations, but each shared the sinuous, natural stylistic conceits, creeping tendrils, vines, and plant life, or what one critic later called "floriated madness." It evolved into Jugendstil in Germany, Stile Liberty in Italy, Vienna Secession in Austria, modernismo in Spain, Bohemian Secession in Eastern Europe, and more. The rich avant-garde style broke from academic as well as baroque, rococo, and other traditions through truly radical departures in type, illustration, page, and poster designs. Art nouveau is an explicit period marker, but in its revived form it helped define the psychedelic style of the 1960s.

BAUHAUS

Among the most progressive early-twentieth –century European design schools, the Staatliches Bauhaus (Weimar from 1919 to 1925, Dessau from 1925 to 1932, and Berlin from 1932 to 1933) was famously antistyle. But the Bauhaus had a philosophy that in its later first home in Weimar and second incarnation in Berlin was a clear visual signature in terms of type, typography, and layout. The look that is most overtly Bauhausian was influenced in part by Russian constructivism and Dutch de Stijl. It was characterized by limited color (usually red and black, though blue was also used) and sans serif typography, usually set in an asymmetrical manner. The typographic style is referred to as quintessentially modern, representative of what **Jan Tschichold** called Elementare Typographie or the New Typography, which became a style of its own.

COMMERCIAL MODERNISM

From the early 1920s through the middle 1930s, L'Art Moderne evolved in the United States into a retooling of product and package called streamlining. Aerodynamics was applied to the veneers of machines and appliances, including automobiles, refrigerators, and vacuum cleaners. Graphically, this took the form of smooth, sleek airbrush rendering. Commercial modernism was the "futuristic" typographic and graphic design manifestation used primarily in the selling —or "styling"—of the goods, akin to (though not exactly) art deco.

CONSTRUCTIVISM

Developed in the Soviet Union in the optimistic wake of the 1917 Bolshevik Revolution, constructivism was an art and architectural movement for the Soviet new society. It touched graphic design in major ways, too, ultimately influencing the Bauhaus and the New Typography. The constructivists, and their productivist offshoots, rejected the idea of art for art's sake as the vestige of the bourgeois class to which previous art had been catered. Its leaders were early proponents of abstract art, and the design of posters and books, while readable, involved abstraction. The term *construction art* was first coined by the painter/poet **Kazimir Malevich** in reference to the designer **Aleksander Rodchenko**, who, in addition to photomontage, used metal type -case materials to build his typographic lay-outs. Heavy bars, stark bold types (both serif and sans), and photomontage are hallmarks. Constructivism can be found in product packaging, logos, posters, book covers, and advertisements. Rodchenko's graphic design works became an inspiration to many Western designers.

DADA

Dada was a nonsense word that signified the twentieth century's first anti-art art movement, from 1916 to 1924, that waged war on the status quo. Dada was affixed to acts of cultural disruption and developed its own metalanguage, which only Dadas could understand. The language appeared in an international review that expressed the Dada gospel through a rambunctious display of expressionism, futurism, cubism, experimental poetry, anarchic imagery, and confrontational manifestos. But ultimately, the overarching character of Dada was forged through its typography. Dada forced the eye to see differently by changing the common perception of the written word, attacking rectilinear conventions of the printed page and breaking apart the sequential order of typeset lines. Italics were thrown in haphaz-ardly, capitals and minuscules were applied at random—all to achieve a disruptive jolt. Dada crusaded against the sanctioned conveyance of meaning by shouting and screaming and thus imitating sound through printed words.

DE STIJL

De Stijl, the Dutch avant-garde design movement, treated pure geometry as something sacred. In 1917, de Stijl emerged as a reductive aesthetic language. The manifesto proclaimed all plastic form derived directly from the rectangle—because it introduced natural order to art—and the three primary colors, plus black. Although rectilinearity was common to all modern movements, for the Dutch it was a matter of faith. **Theo van Doesburg** (born Christian E.M. Küpper), **Vilmos Huszar, Antony Kok, Bart van der Leck, Piet Mondrian,** and **J.J.P. Oud** founded the group. Van Doesburg edited and designed its journal, *de Stijl*, and through its frequently mutating format was an innovator of modern graphic design. The logo for the early issues of *de Stijl* was designed from rectangular patterns arranged on a strict grid and had an emblematic blocky appearance. Van Doesburg defined type design and typography as the offspring of straight lines and rectilinear geometry.

EXPRESSIONISM

German expressionism was founded in 1905. Later, two expressionist groups, **Die Brücke** in 1905 and **Der Blaue Reiter** in 1912, emerged. The former was engaged in figuration and the latter in abstraction. The offspring of their collective radicalism is a visual language influenced by primitive iconography, including African totems and masks. Expressionists preferred the woodcut, a medium that resists perfection, because the hard surface was resistant to any forms of subtlety. Woodblocks required that artists violently gouge the wood to make their marks—they were forced to struggle, which in turn allowed the artists to reveal their emotions, resulting in rawness that stripped the respective subjects to their primal states. Deformation of the figure was employed to heighten the intensity of expression. Prior to World

War I, expressionism attacked the status quo mostly in metaphysical terms. After 1918, following the November Revolution that installed a republic in war-ravaged Imperial Germany, many in the movement became more fervently political, allying themselves with Socialist and Communist parties. The raw graphic style they adopted from expressionism stripped away both artifice and propriety with the goal of creating formal visual language of the revolution. The expressionists did not produce commercial typefaces, but they did influence others.

FASCIST

Take one part L'Art Moderne, two parts heroic, along with a dollop of futurist lettering, and the result would be youth-oriented Italian Fascist styling. Although not the sole style of the Fascist Party and state, it was the primary visual signature for a movement that aimed its allure at youth culture. The airbrush quality and kinetic type style of Fascism is direct but without the sledgehammer approach of faux Italian classicism, which sought to promote the party as the vanguard of the new Roman Empire. Instead, this style was rather inspirational.

FUTURISM

Italian futurism was a cultural insurgency that insisted art and design were inextricably linked to machine-age technology; the graphic style that best expressed their ideology was a noisy, dissonant cacophony of letters, types, and words that was a curious mixture of archaic letterforms and futuristic compositions. **Filippo T. Marinetti's** *First Futurist Manifesto*, published in 1909, was a paean to progress and a call to arms. Futurist manifestos were written in impassioned prose and composed in bombastic layouts with type that exploded on the printed page. Futurism was a radical shift in type and layout from reliance on staid central axis composition to dynamic asymmetry. Typeset and hand-drawn letterforms were no longer quietly or elegantly printed on a page; they were transformed into vibrant onomatopoeia. The goal was to recast language by eliminating conventional grammar and syntax, and this was manifest in the invention of his most emblematic visual/verbal poetic form, parole in liberta (words-in-freedom), which he created specifically to express notions of speed through a compositional economy of means.

HEROIC

Heroic style, found in almost all countries, idealizes the common man and beatifies the common leader. For centuries, graphic propagandists have created icons extolling fake strengths and false virtues. Heroic representation is a pose—credible myths and acceptable legends. A heroic figure, such as the lock-jawed, broad-shouldered humannequins devised by the German poster artist **Ludwig Hohlwein** (1874–1949), forged indelible bonds with the audience. Realism is the primary trope, and this involves romanticizing those depicted in such a way that what remains is a heroic shell. Heroic realism recalls the icons of ancient Rome. Yet every period is replete with its own heroic imagery conforming to specific needs. Whether called socialist realism, national socialist realism, heroic realism, or just plain realism, the all-heroic imagery is designed to achieve the same effect. **Elbert Hubbard**, founder of the Roycrofters, said, "The heroic man does not pose; he leaves that for the man who wishes to be thought heroic."

INTERNATIONAL STYLE

Until the mid-1960s, the international style was big "D" design. The most ubiquitous graphic design in the United States and Europe was based on the modern Swiss grid. Then came the sixties, a confluence of radical politics and youth culture—a reassessment of sacred canon leading to a purposeful rejection of the old order, which in terms of design was, curiously, modernism. Some say that 1965 was the year that the modern became old fashioned, not only causing semantic confusion but forcing proponents to reassess their life's work. In fact, modernism was in such a state of flux during that time that the postmodern nomenclature had to be coined in the early 1970s so that art historians and cultural pundits had some means of describing the ensuing disquiet and the next evolutionary stage.

MODERNISM

The term *modern* literally means "up to date" and has been used to describe fashionable artworks and movements, but modernism specifically refers to the progressive design period between the two World Wars—the age of L'Esprit Nouveau, the Bauhaus, and de Stijl. The masters of orthodox modernism vehemently denied that their reductive and functional art and design was a style; rather, it was a way of life, an ethical and moral system. It was a purposeful rejection of bourgeois historicism and sentimentalism that dominated European design until the early twentieth century. But it did have common denominators and a look. Modernists challenged prevailing aesthetics and beliefs with reductivist principles. Simplicity, asymmetry, and minimalism were among the common traits that dictated white space and sans serif type. That was the beginning. European modernism evolved into what **Philip Johnson** and **Henry-Russell Hitchcock** called the international style, exerting influence in architecture, furniture, and graphic design. The prevailing style of multinational corporations was simplicity, which made international communications more legible and comprehensible.

NEW TYPOGRAPHY

By the 1920s, a reevaluation of typographic and layout standards occurred when designers practicing the New Typography embraced classical ideals of legibility yet, reflecting on their contemporary, machine-age times, opted for a change in typographic methodologies. The young **Jan Tschichold**, a German type designer who codified the new style, led this movement. Central axis composition, for example, was rejected in favor of asymmetry, but even more significant was the mission of these "modern" designers to expunge the mediocre, the vernacular types and typographies that appeared on signs, bills, and advertisements, which represented rote rather than sophisticated design thinking. The New Typography was both a language and style that proffered reductive or "elementary" methods. Its goal was universality, but its rationalism appealed to the needs of only certain kinds of businesses and corporations. Strict grids and austere sans serif typefaces were not always appropriate for, say, a milk carton, detergent package, or supermarket sign that demanded stark, sometimes crass eye-catching immediacy to capture a consumer's attention. But the New Typography attempted to influence them all.

POSTMODERN

After modernism, then what? Postmodern (PM) graphic design emerged roughly in the mid-80s, reached its stylistic zenith during the late-90s, and was characterized by stylistic eclecticism. It started before the computer but derives much of its thrust from the Macintosh revolution that spawned the first wave of digital type design and later ad hoc fontography. An academic style, it integrated theory, politics, and social relations into design practice and by extension influenced the typographical fashion of the moment: deconstruction. This was an intellectual approach of analyzing texts introduced by poststructuralist critic **Jacques Derrida** that challenged the receiver of visual and textual messages to comprehend the complexity of meaning. Layering, distortion, and density are PM traits created as much to emote as to be read. Postmodern was not monolithic. Other groupings of styles were welcome in the big tent. Proponents of new wave (which **Gary Panter** called "sterilized punk"), grunge, post-punk, retro pastiche, and vernacular took pains to throw off the yoke (or grid) that Swiss modernism had imposed since the early fifties. PM promoted complexity over simplicity, objectivity routing subjectivity, and ornament defeating austerity.

PSYCHEDELIC

During the late 1960s, the psychedelic style grew out of the hippie counterculture, which hailed hallucinogenic drugs and rock. Characterized by seemingly illegible typefaces, vibrating colors, and vintage illustrations, psychedelic art was a rebellious graphic language created to communicate with an exclusive community and for a short time excluded all others until it was adopted as the youth culture code. The overall psychedelic visual language was composed of a fairly consistent assortment of recurring elements: Public domain images, including engravings, old photos, labels, postcards, and other commercial ephemera, were frequently used. Custom psychedelic typefaces were hand drawn based on Victorian and art nouveau models—everything that was passé was inherently antiestablishment. There were layers of graphic effluvia common to all psychedelic art, yet the compositions were often strategically arranged and obsessively sketched—nothing was left to chance. Although being stoned may have added to the enjoyment of psychedelic posters, it wasn't altogether necessary. Certain art and design tenets were rejected, but once the new ones were learned, the work was perfectly legible and accessible.

PUNK

Like Dada, punk (or its contemporary, grunge) is authentic anti-design design. Purposefully ad hoc, the style represents a deliberate rejection of graphic design rules. The term *punk*, which denotes petty thugs and jailhouse paramours, is echoed by graphics meant to be dirty and uncouth—a violent rejection of pseudo-psychedelic hippie pop. There are various punk strains with different design signatures. English punks argue that their ransom note and magic marker graphics are free of any professional contamination and more like Dada. Yet there are plenty of punk albums, periodicals, and posters that conform to at least a small semblance of conventional techniques. The devices that gave punk its look—cut-out letters, ripped clothing, safety pins, and Day-Glo—quickly became design clichés, like psychedelia, either co-opted or happily adopted by the mainstream.

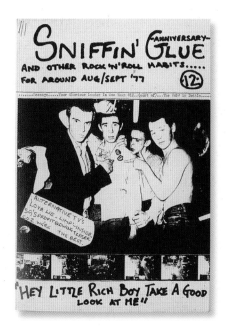

RETRO

Retro (or pastiche) is the act of reusing timeworn stylistic mannerisms as part of contemporary graphic design. The retro use of any accepted style is an effortless way to establish familiar graphic codes with limited risk. Retro can give new products instant heritage and old ones an opportunity to flag their authenticity, even where it does not exist. Retro is one of the more dependable tools for sparking a certain kind of consumer interest in certain products by saying something is old yet new—combining vintage values and current attitudes. Arguably, retro is not a design style but a marketing term invented by retailers, a catchall used to label products inspired by the past (one hundred or ten years ago) and to inveigle their products into the consumers' consciousness. Nonetheless, drawing from historical references is not only a pejorative—rather than rob the design tombs, some designers integrate historical forms into their respective styles.

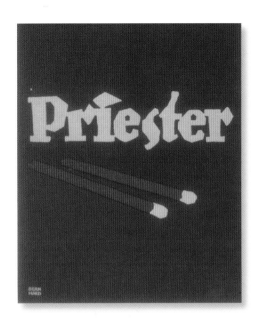

SACHPLAKAT

An early-twentieth-century advertising poster genre in Germany known as *plakatstil* (poster style) was the umbrella for a submovement known for extreme simplicity known as *sachplakat* (object poster). Sachplakat's acknowledged inventor was an eighteen-year-old named **Lucian Bernhard** who, in 1906, entered a poster competition sponsored by Berlin's Priester Match Company. His first sketch was typically art nouveau (or jugendstil): It included a cigar in an ashtray on a checked tablecloth with dancing nymphets formed by the intertwining tobacco smoke. Next to the ashtray were two wooden matches. A friend mistakenly complimented Bernhard on the excellent cigar advertisement, which forced him to rethink the composition and, one after another, he began eliminating everything but the two matches, which were enlarged, painted in red with yellow tips, and placed on a dark maroon field. At the top of the image area he lettered "Priester" by hand in bold block letters—simplicity personified—and sachplakat was born. Art nouveau met its demise not because of Bernhard's accidental invention, but because visual complexity no longer achieved the desired results.

SOCIAL AND SOCIALIST REALISM

In 1934, Stalin and author **Maxim Gorky** devised a new doctrine called socialist realism. It started as a literary decree but quickly influenced the visual arts as well. Socialist realism rejected formalism as bourgeois influences on art. It abolished all works of art (and eventually persecuted all artists) that were suspected of harboring personal creative agendas. Ironically, what replaced abstraction was a romantic and heroic worldview not all that pictorially different from American social realism's murals that celebrated the worker, labor, and industry. But unlike American social realism fostered by the government, socialist realism was imposed upon all Soviet artists, who were forced to belong to sanctioned artists' unions. True realists, naturalists, impressionists—those accused of being aloof from the daily struggle of the proletariat—were removed from artistic life. Soviet art historian and critic **Vladimir Kemenov** said, "Soviet artists present the wholesome and integral art of socialist realism, expressed in profound artistic images reflecting true life, showing the struggle between the old and the new and the inevitable triumph of the new and progressive, an art mobilizing Soviet people for further victories." Socialist realism, which included graphic design and photography based on detailed, faux realistic depiction, took the edges off the grit of reality, providing instead an ideal or heroic vision.

STREAMLINE

Streamline was a distinctly American modern design style that began during the 1920s and 1930s. It is often confused with art deco, which shared some of its visual characteristics. Streamline introduced the industrial designer. In an effort to stimulate consumption, they crusaded against outmoded industrial output that resulted in the application of new futuristic veneers signaling the machine-made attributes of products and commodities. Influenced by modern art, which to a certain degree was inspired by the machine itself, the industrial designer was not rebelling against mass production, but rather embraced it. Streamlining was built on aerodynamic principles; for this reason, the teardrop shape derived because it allowed for more rapid movement. Modernistic graphics, characterized by sleek airbrushed veneers, framed and "dressed," were otherwise quaint and timeworn products. Marketing strategists developed the illusion of progress by using type and images that were seductively progressive, or what the industrial designer **Raymond Loewy** called MAYA, "most advanced yet acceptable."

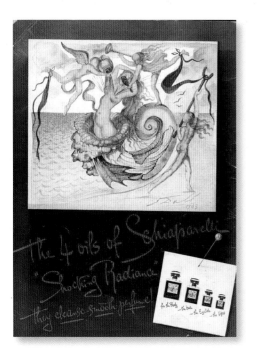

SURREALISM

Surrealism was a liberation of the unconscious activity of the mind. In 1924, it began as a literary style that involved automatic or subconscious writing, but soon the dreamlike language of surrealism was manifest in pictorial art. Surrealism induced physical and mental vertigo that both stimulated and sabotaged perception. Surrealistic imagery had been used without the label in the popular arts since the mid-nineteenth century. The macabre, dreamlike cartoons by French caricaturist **J.J. Grandville**, circa 1850, prefigured contemporary science-fiction art and surrealistic musings. By the late 1930s, surrealism had become a common trope for many commercial artists in various disciplines. Both mysterious and accessible, surrealism provided a modern means to visually express complex as well as simplistic ideas. The art critic **Lucy Lippard** calls surrealism "house broken Dada . . . Northern fantasy subjected to French lucidity." As commercial art, surrealism was a benign tool used for advertising perfumes and cosmetics, not a revolutionary language.

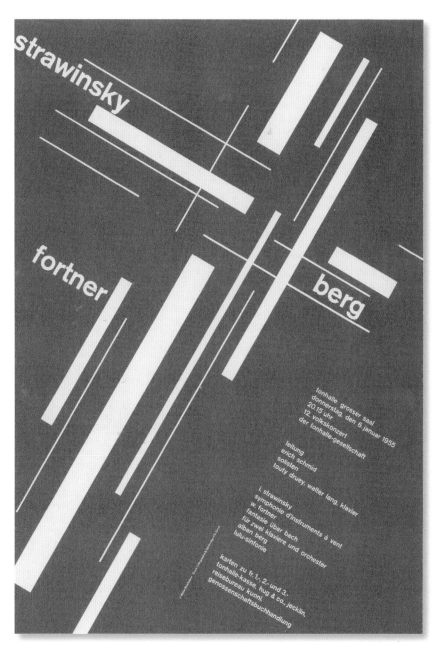

SWISS

The Swiss School, or International Typographic Style, which emerged in the late 1940s, absorbed aspects of de Stijl, the Bauhaus, and the New Typography. Its philosophical goal to achieve objective clarity through graphic design evolved into a common graphic language of businesses worldwide. Swiss layouts were constructed of pure geometric elements and organized mathematically on a grid. Akzidenz-Grotesk type (a well-proportioned late-nineteenth-century sans serif typeface), flush left and ragged right settings, and paragraphs indicated by an "interval space" instead of the conventional paragraph indent were key components of the International Typographic Style. It was also laden with strict typographic hierarchies and spacial considerations wherein only one type style (in one or two weights) served all the basic informational and navigational needs in the same layout. Relative importance was shown through changes in point size or weight and the position of the type on the grid. Invisible grids had long been present in classical design, but the overt application of modular units, geometric progressions, and mathematical sequences were laid down as strict rules. Sans serif type was the most emblematic component of the International Typographic Style. In 1954, **Adrian Frutiger** designed Univers (the name presumed its universal adoption in English-speaking countries), a mathematically constructed and visually programmed family with twenty-one variations (expanded, bold, condensed, etc.) indicated by number. In 1956, **Edouard Hoffman** decided that it was time to refine Akzidenz-Grotesk and collaborated with **Max Miedinger** on a well-defined sans serif known as Neue Haas Grotesk (so named for the Hass type foundry in Switzerland). When it was produced in Germany by D. Stempel foundry in 1961, the name was surprisingly changed to Helvetica.

VICTORIAN

The Victorian era from 1837 to 1901 marked a span of eclectic design that exerted profound influence on graphics the world over. The term *Victorian* and all the stylistic manifestations it came to represent was not, however, exclusive to England but was used to describe analogous historical revivals in Europe and the United States during the second half of the nineteenth century. Graphic design (though not yet referred to as such) was an assimilation of Byzantine, Romanesque, and rococo sensibilities, drowning in excessive revivalist ornamentation that was both quaint and exciting. Typeface and page design reveled in ornamental flourish that directly related to architectural aesthetics. Graphic stylists—from job printers to bookmakers—appropriated the decorative tropes of Victorian facades and monuments. Magazine and newspaper illustrations were minutely detailed with ornate filigrees often in which typefaces and customized lettering appeared to be carved as though in stone. Considering the cumbersome wood and metal engraving techniques necessary to create these eccentric concoctions, the results are remarkably and intricately precise. Printers worked with the standard metal and wood types, but if they didn't have enough of one font they didn't think twice about including others together on one line or composition. The Victorian style of disparate faces on a single page derives from this banal necessity.

VERNACULAR

Vernacular is simply a common language that we all know. In graphic design, vernacular broadly refers to what was once called everyday "commercial art," including signage, packaging, advertisements, publications, and so on, that constitute quotidian "mass culture." There are many vernacular accents: A Tide detergent box, for instance, did not become the quintessential package design that it is through Darwinian natural selection, but rather, because its type and decorative motif have been impressed upon mass consciousness through repeated promotion and display. The Tide detergent package is so commonplace today that it is often copied and parodied. Vernacular was a word, not a style, until in the late 1980s when **Tibor Kalman** used untutored, retrofitted typography for sophisticated design projects. By embracing what was once considered crass as part of the design discourse, Kalman elevated commonplace layout to the exceptional artifact. Vernacular may be considered a subset of retro—the revival of what was once everyday, making it more rarified, if only for the moment.

Hava Sm

Matter
= *the measure {of love}*
SPIRIT
MOUNS
NEVER
STEEL

NELLA SCU

www.IrvingFarm.com
ROASTED
Coffee Company
New York
Irving Farm C
Millerton, N
www.IrvingFarm.com
ROASTED
Coffee Company
New York
Irving Farm C
Millerton, N

CIGARROS PUROS SUPERIORES
SUPERIOR CIGARS MANFD
OF THE FINEST
VUELTA ABAJO TABACOS.
FLOR EXTRA FINA

PLAYING WITH

OLD
—NEW—
STYLE

Young designers are always amazed when they learn graphic design is historically rooted in styles that define certain periods—and that there are so many of them too. Graphic styles are composed of the good, bad, and ugly—and often the bad and ugly are the most popular. In this section of exercises, the goal is to suspend value judgments in terms of what style was best and worst, but rather to adopt, adapt, and interpret all of them as parts of your own graphic design voice. The outcome of each exercise may not (and probably will not) mean you are committed to a particular style, but it will enable you to appreciate the stylistic tools at your disposal. It will also, one hopes, allow you to mix and match, to create hybrids that may evolve into a personal approach or style. Now, let the play begin.

Create an album cover that parodies famous 1920s Russian avant-garde design using a photo of yourself.

STYLE: **RUSSIAN CONSTRUCTIVISM**

EXERCISE STEPS:

1. Select a black-and-white photo of yourself and remove the background.

2. Choose typefaces that reflect the spirit of the style.

    a. Limit yourself to six typefaces.
    b. Mix and match the types to give a raw quality.

3. Combine the type image and image into a collage or montage against a contrasting background.

4. Add elements to give your character a unique twist.

5. Add color and shading to give it an antique or distressed appearance.

TITLE: *Gonwards*
DESIGNER: Andrew Swainson

Andy Partridge wanted to create a pitch-perfect, yet witty reinterpretation of a rare, typographically raucous, 1930 Russian constructivist book cover composed by avant-gardist Solomon Telingater. Andrew Swainson, of London's Cactus, designed *Gonwards*, a CD box set of songs by American expat Peter Blegvad and Partridge with the aim of making it old and new at the same time. The front was printed in trompe-l'oeil fashion that simulated indications of wear and tear, so the entire package appears a little soiled, like a vintage orange Kodak film box. "I thought it was rough, beautiful, modern," Blegvad says of the design. "I saw the potential of having our titles in place of the Russian type on the front and of Peter's head and mine replacing Kirsanov [the photo on the original]. I liked the damage on the one I saw." It reminded him of various graphic boxes he admired, "such as matchbox labels with disparate typography, out-of-register printing, dreamlike, cartoon-like images that seem oddly noble."

PLAYFUL TIP:

See how far you can stretch the original style while maintaining the look and feel of the original.

....

1. Change colors.

2. Alter typefaces.

3. Rearrange the elements to create a completely different composition.

4. Create a hybrid of constructivism and something else.

5. Try it with more than one photo.

Opposite/This Page
Inspiration: Solomon Telingator, 1930.

№2

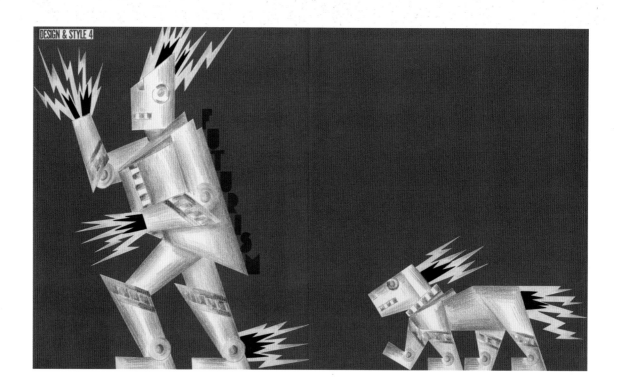

Create "tour guides" for different historical styles, featuring historical and contemporary applications.

STYLES: **JUGENDSTIL, ART DECO, SURREALISM, FUTURISM, BAUHAUS, STREAMLINE**

EXERCISE STEPS:

1. Select three distinct graphic styles.

2. Collect twenty examples of each style in graphic design, type, furniture, fashion, and architecture.

3. Write a brief interpretative history of the styles showing how they have influenced contemporary design. Long captions are acceptable. A timeline would be useful for the reader.

4. Design each guide in the style being featured.

5. Publish.

TITLE: *Design and Style*
DESIGNER: Seymour Chwast

This series of booklets was produced for Mohawk Paper Mills to exhibit the variety of paper weights and styles. Design history through the lens of style was focal. Key or iconic examples of each style were shown, often highlighted by intricate paper special effects. Seymour Chwast designed each cover as an interpretation (not a copy) of the respective style, adding his own quirky twist to the visual impact of the project.

DE STIJL

DESIGN & STYLES

Nº 3

Redesign an existing mass-market coffee package to make it more appealing to an upscale consumer.

STYLES: **VICTORIAN, ART DECO**

EXERCISE STEPS:

1. Select a popular brand (Nescafé, Folgers, Starbucks, etc.).

2. Sketch out alternative bag and/or tin designs (but leave the logo alone).

3. Conceive a name that will set this brand apart as "premium."

4. Design two different kinds of packages for two different coffee options.

5. Create ancillary products (cup, napkins, cup holder).

TITLE: Irving Farm
DESIGNER: Louise Fili

Irving Farm sells coffee beans from around the world. It also has a store that sells its own coffee and pastries. The original bag design was not demonstrative enough. Louise Fili designed a prosaic visual environ that combined nineteenth-century decorative graphics with 1930s typography and mixed it together with a contemporary color palette. The two different styles of bags represented an upgrade of the product, and the stamps were used to indicate which bean was in the package.

№4

Touch the heart of an acquaintance through a designed gift.

STYLES: **ART DECO, VERNACULAR**

EXERCISE STEPS:

1. With the freedom to create a gift using a 1920s commercial style, you select a game. The point is for someone you know well to be surprised and happy. Determine what game you want to make and play.

2. Select elements of the style that are most appropriate to frame or package this game.

3. Conceive a name for the product.

4. Sketch on tracing paper or computer screen variations of a logo and/or primary image.

5. Use the computer to design two or three variations of the game box, instruction guide, and pieces.

6. Apply your outcome to a prototype.

7. Finalize the project by making a real box and game components.

TITLE: Mercado Social Club
DESIGNER: Bridget Dearborn

In Touch Someone's Heart, a class taught by Stefan Sagmeister in the MFA Design/Designer as Author + Entrepreneur program at the School of Visual Arts, Bridget Dearborn's assignment was to create a designed object that could touch the heart of someone she knew. "I live in an apartment building in Brooklyn," Dearborn explains, "and I am friendly with all of my neighbors. Directly below me lives Miguel Mercado, originally from Puerto Rico and now in his mid-seventies. He has been hosting a weekly dominoes game in his kitchen for over twenty-five years. I decided that I would make a special set of dominoes for him, branded as if he had his own social club." Dearborn specifically took as inspiration artifacts from the golden (or pre-Castro) era of Cuban graphic style, especially the cigar boxes, which have become the vernacular of this genre. "The typography, the palette, and the patterns used in this style capture perfectly the energy of this group of friends who have played together for so long."

Belinda ›
CIGAR LABEL
— DATE UNKNOWN —

‿ Havana Smoker
CIGAR LABEL
— DATE UNKNOWN —

NOTE:

Using art deco limits what game you will produce. It should not be too high-tech or low-tech, but rather something that might have been common during the period when art deco was fashionable (1920s to early 1930s).

....

1. Research the games and their packages from this period of time.

2. Board games were very popular, as were checkers and dominoes.

Inspirations: Original tobacco labels, c. 1900.

EVERY
Saturday
NIGHT

EVERY *Saturday* NIGHT

every
SATURDAY
NIGHT

SATURDAYS in BROOKLYN

SATURDAYS IN BROOKLYN

social club

EVERY *Saturday* NIGHT

social club

MERCADO
social club

MERCADO
social   club

SOCIAL CLUB

social club

SOCIAL CLUB

SOCIAL CLUB

Invent a beverage company that is represented by a venerable heritage, yet is of the moment, and design the label for its signature product.

STYLES: **CLASSIC, CARIBBEAN, FRENCH MODERN**

EXERCISE STEPS:

1. Select a product (e.g., rum, beer, soda).

2. Create a name that represents its fictitious origins.

3. Determine the type or shape of bottle or can.

4. Choose stock historical imagery or render your own imagery that telegraphs the name.

5. Design a label and promotional display.

TITLE: 10 Cane Brand
DESIGNER: Werner Design Werks

Working closely with the Moët Hennessy's new concepts team, Werner Design Werks developed the 10 Cane Brand, made specifically for mixing premium cocktails. "The essence of the creative direction was the single word *alchemy*," says Sharon Werner, whose team developed names, brand stories, and packaging directions that all incorporated alchemy in various ways. Two images drove home the concept, a Marcel Wanders plate and a Custo Barcelona photograph, which spoke to the spirit of alchemy. The visual inspiration was interpreted "by mixing an elegant and classic crest with an irreverently placed label." The crest, which is nearly obliterated, depicts the monkeys that roam the island of Trinidad, and the ten stalks of crossed cane define the number of sugar canes pressed into each bottle of 10 Cane. Foliage intermingles with traditional heraldic iconography and *Saccharum Officinarum,* which simply means "sugarcane."

PLAYFUL TIP:

Many liquor and soft drink brands are based on real and imagined legacies.

1. Avoid making something that is too common or overused.

2. Review the competition.

3. Develop something familiar yet different from the rest.

Typographically make advertisements or promotions for something using American wood type.

STYLE: **VICTORIAN**

EXERCISE STEPS:

1. Read about the history of wood type in Rob Roy Kelly's *American Wood Type, 1828–1900: Notes on the Evolution of Decorated and Large Types and Comments on Related Trades of the Period* (a Da Capo paperback).

2. For samples of vintage faces, reference Carol Belanger Grafton's *Bizarre & Ornamental Alphabets (Lettering, Calligraphy, Typography)* (Dover Books).

3. For original samples, visit your local flea market and you may find actual wood typefaces that can be used to make impressions.

4. Scan different styles into your computer and then mix them in a single word or sentence.

5. Write a clever or pithy headline that expresses what you want to say and then find typefaces that "illustrate" the headline.

6. Make multiple versions of each composition using different faces and colors.

7. As a playful challenge, see if you can make the layout appear old and new at the same time.

TITLE: The Long Island Rail Road Company
DESIGNER: Bruce Viemeister

Bruce Viemeister was inspired by the old signage used during the mid-1800s, when the line was used for extensive travel and exploration, rather than day-to-day commuting. However, he took a more contemporaneous direction with both type and color. While suggesting a mid-nineteenth-century sensibility, the design is undeniably contemporary. "My hope is that the style of this package will bring forward those past experiences and evoke a sense of excitement in the story that remains along the Long Island Rail Road," he says.

VISIT THE
AFRICAN AMERICAN
HEMPSTEAD

LEARN ABOUT THE PAST
Amityville's
HISTORICAL

LAUDER

LEARN AT T
american
**AIR POWER
MUSEUM**
FARMINGDALE

Combine vintage and contemporary styles to personalize a beer brand.

STYLE: **AMERICAN VICTORIAN**

EXERCISE STEPS:

1. Determine what story you want to tell about your product through typography.

2. Conceive the name of the beer you want to brand or rebrand.

3. Select a typeface from a wood type source that is condensed enough to fit on a label but is still readable.

4. Bottles are not flat, so your design should conform to the contours of the surface.

5. Sketch with pencil various iterations of your label. You are not making a logo, per se, but a title that will be iconic.

6. Avoid your label looking retro by adding a contemporary or futuristic element.

7. Print out the label in color on a laser printer, cut it out with a knife or scissors, and affix it to your bottle.

TITLE: IPA Del Rey
DESIGNER: Timothy Cohan

For this special label and package for IPA beer, Timothy Cohan illustrated the label and hand lettered the typography. "The illustration is a view of the LA beach from my former office window," he says. "The portrait on the neck of the bottle is a former colleague and (still) friend of mine, who was the target audience in this assignment." Beer identities often blend old and new to suggest heritage on the one hand and contemporary attributes on the other. Although Cohan's typography has a retro or vintage aesthetic, and the shape of the label has a classic feel, the fusion of hand lettering and loose drawing speaks to the present. Cohan says the approach he devised also speaks "in my voice." Neo-Victorian lettering is used for the brand name, with homespun illustration emphasizing the artisanal quality of the brew. The typography is at once newly designed in a vintage style, giving the consumer the sense the beer has been in existence a long time.

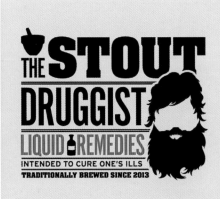

TITLE: The Stout Druggist (Liquid Cures)

DESIGNER: Kathie Alexander

The Stout Druggist beer brand is a dream, says Kathie Alexander, "that someday we will wake up from a night of fun feeling better and not worse. Having a good time but doing something good for your body. People are always looking for new ways to stay healthy. In a world where most food/drink is being questioned for safety, it's nice to know that you can still relax with beer that's good for you." She took the classic beer package and integrated the vintage elements with modern design:

VINTAGE:

- Druggist, a word used in vintage advertisement
- A picture of a druggist
- The diamond-shaped label
- Aged background color instead of white
- Ornate borders and illustrations
- Detailed illustrations rather than photography

MODERN:

- Metallic background
- Vibrant colors
- Picture of a hipster

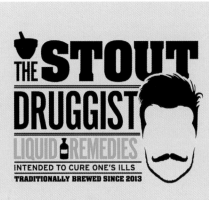

PLAYFUL TIP:

1. Select a bottle color that complements your label colors.

2. Use a real bottle.

3. Make multiples to see how they appear in a row.

Using the visual languages common to beer packaging and drugstore remedies, this hybrid version has its own character.

8

Create the identity—logo, signage, menus, and matches— for a restaurant that has a vintage French bistro theme.

STYLES: **FRENCH CAFÉ, ORNAMENTAL, VICTORIAN**

EXERCISE STEPS:

1. Photograph a storefront in your neighborhood. You will use that as your point of departure.

2. Give your bistro a name and design the logo.

3. Develop your setting—add tables, awnings, and so on, to the storefront.

4. Determine your fare and design a menu.

5. Design all the ancillaries (dinnerware, napkins, matches, business card, and so on).

TITLE: Parc

DESIGNER: Mucca/Matteo Bologna

The identity for Parc is a tribute to French café culture, serving traditional bistro fare in Philadelphia's Rittenhouse Square. "We developed the logo design from an original period typeface," says Matteo Bologna, "and an authentically eclectic mix of historical typography for the menus. The exterior signage and outdoor service area are designed to reflect Parc's accessible elegance. The venue's proximity to the green space also inspired lighthearted references to the park-dwelling creatures nearby—silhouettes of pigeons and squirrels adorn the menus."

Brasserie

PARC

Bistro

227 SOUTH 18TH STREET ~ PHILADELPHIA PA ~ 19103

9

Conceive and design the packaging for a stationery product that has a vintage veneer yet is a useful gift today.

STYLE: **ITALIAN ART DECO**

EXERCISE STEPS:

1. Identify an item, such as pencils, paper clips, or glue, that would benefit from a fresh yet vintage style of package.

2. Make an outline indicating the dimensions of the package front, back, sides, and interior.

3. Create a product name and other wording for the package.

4. Design one or more motifs.

5. Create a final virtual composite showing all sides of package.

TITLE: Perfetto
DESIGNER: Louise Fili

For a designer as passionate about "all things Italian" as Louise Fili, it is not a leap from designing books and restaurants to creating products, such as the Perfetto pencils. Drawing on her large library of Italian art deco typefaces and other printing material, this product has the look and feel of vintage pencil boxes combined with other 1930s Italian consumables.

Use Italian commercial typographic references to make an artist's book.

STYLE: **VERNACULAR**

Roseto Comunale

VIALE DEL CIRCO MASSIMO
HOURS: Mon–Sun 8am–6.30pm

THE ROSETO COMUNALE IS a lovely place
to talk a walk through. The aroma of the
roses is incredible as well as the beauty of
the flowers accompanying it.

Look for the typography made from roses.

EXERCISE STEPS:

1. Visit Rome (or any Italian city where typography is found). If you can't do that, then research art and images from Italy.

2. Photograph or scan everyday ephemera, signs, and packages.

3. Crop the images to focus on the most interesting or quirky aspect of the typography.

4. Juxtapose contrasting or complementary types and typography.

5. Use these "collages" as the basis for page compositions.

6. Design a cover.

TITLE: *The Typography Lover's Guide to Roma*
DESIGNER: Janine Toro

During SVA's Masters Workshop: Design & Typography in Rome, Janine Toro was inspired by the history of Italian graphics and graphic design. She incorporated classical, commercial, vernacular, and artistic references into the design of note cards, with the goal of producing printed souvenirs that take the user through Rome via its typography while at the same time exploring the food, culture, and design. Toro used for the box an orange wrapper she found in a Roman green market. She made a card with a piece of wrapping paper from Volpetti, a famous cheese and salami shop. And for Cartolerio Pantheon, a close-up of a vintage calligraphy manual was just the right touch. Although Toro's artifacts were vintage, the overall look and feel of the boxed set was entirely contemporary.

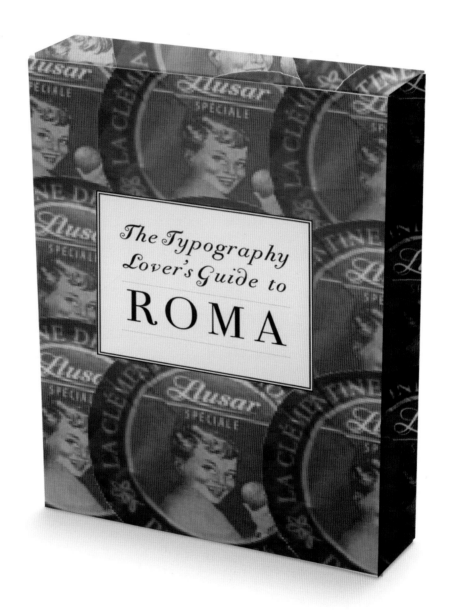

PLAYING WITH VISUAL

VOICE

We all have a certain tone, timbre, and accent in our speaking voices—so, too, in our design and visual voices. This is determined by many factors, from the nuanced gestures to the broad strokes. It comes from the typefaces we use and the scale of imagery. Call it preference or taste, invariably design cannot be entirely neutral. Historical styles contribute to the personal visual voice. How they are used contributes to the accent and language that we use to express messages. Not all design can have an operatic personal voice, but there is always a little noise that belongs to the designer in virtually everything that is designed.

№11

Use cut-and-paste collage to mash up multiple styles and images into a cohesive visual statement on a specific theme.

STYLES: **ART DECO, MODERN, SURREALISM, VERNACULAR**

TITLE: *Storied Sips*
DESIGNER: Poul Lange

Poul Lange says he has always been inspired by everyday graphics: the labels of foods and beverages, magazine ads, street signage, and advertisement posters. "Of course, every paper scrap is not created equal, and in my eyes there are eras that hold much more graphic promise than others. When I got this assignment," he notes, "I soon realized that the important periods of mixology overlap some of my favorite graphic movements—from the letterpress typography of the 1880s (Old Fashioned), over 1930s art deco (Hemingway Daiquiri), to the fabulous mid-century modern (Martini)—it was the perfect opportunity for me to dig into my archive of vintage paper, magazines, postcards, maps, photos, and labels. In my collages, I always try to stay true to the media, use the original material, and stay away from Photoshop as much as possible. So the originals are put together with glue, and most of the paper is way older than me. But like a fine wine (or whiskey), I feel that these precious scraps only improve with age and look even better if they are a bit frayed around the edges."

EXERCISE STEPS:

1. Gather a collection of scraps and cutouts from vintage books and magazines.

2. Make certain you use only copyright-free materials or undefined portions of larger work. (Most vintage product labels and many vintage advertisements are possible.)

3. Compose these snippets into a legible and readable composition that conforms to a specific theme, story, or plot for a book or magazine.

FINE

AN IDEAL INVIGORATOR.

TRADE MARK

VODKA

Spiritueux

Champagne

Cognac

RHUM

BOURBON

GIN

TEQUILA

VERMOUTH

LIQUEURS

MARASCHINO

WHISKY.

ABSINTHE

Your eyes feel *refreshed*.

RUM

TRADER VIC'S

MAI TAI

59

Transform a souvenir postcard into social protest.

STYLE: **AMERICAN VERNACULAR**

EXERCISE STEPS:

1. Collect examples of souvenir postcards from souvenir vendors or antique shops. There are many that sell them for very little.

2. Find the source material that best suits the irony of your message.

3. Trace the type or lettering that will express your message.

4. Draw or collage images that suggest the original while conveying the message.

5. Do not just copy the original. Add hints of wit and humor—the original is a point of reference for the receiver of the message.

TITLE: *Save Us from Their Paradise;*
Together We Can End Child Sex Tourism
DESIGNER: Andrew Seetoh

This project was designed to reconceive familiar, vernacular imagery—illustrated, typographical souvenir postcards—to communicate to a contemporary audience of concerned citizens a message of social importance. Using classic shaded lettering as his focal point, Andrew Seetoh transformed a vintage travel postcard into a poignant statement with an ironic twist. "From afar it looks like another typically happy 'wish you were here' travel postcard," Seetoh explains, "but as you peer into the word Paradise you see the horrible image of sex slavery. I wanted to go with 'Vus Sea,' which was an unscrambled code for 'Save Us,' but in the end I decided to go for a more direct approach."

THE TRICK:

It is important when choosing a fairly familiar graphic style for a targeted message to make certain your audience understands the stylistic reference. Select an approach that will avoid ambiguity and enforce the idea of the piece. Also, your reference should not be obscure.

1. Show your visual ideas to someone before committing it to print.

2. Sleep on it to make sure it still appeals to you in the morning.

Repurpose Soviet agitprop posters to celebrate something entirely contemporary.

STYLE: **SOCIALIST REALISM**

EXERCISE STEPS:

1. Study the collections of old Soviet posters from the 1930s, 1940s, and 1950s.

2. Select three posters and copy them.

3. Make variations of each layout, keeping in mind that a subtle twist will change the meaning.

4. Retain as much of the original as needed for it to be recognizable.

5. Alter the image and replace the type with your own concept.

TITLE: *Propaganda*
DESIGNER: Carlo Miccio

Propaganda is made of digitally manipulated Soviet propaganda posters, where the original texts have been changed into new slogans inviting the masses to fall in love, to search for wisdom in sex/eros, and believe beauty is revolutionary.

The source images are legally recycled from the Internet and assembled using digital software. For the catchphrases, Miccio uses "Cyrillic-like fonts," which can be easily read when in English or Italian. "I avoided using images from the Stalin era, when the propaganda posters become instrumental in enhancing the cult of personality, as well as establishing the gray rhetoric of the Brezhnev years. This later language was very different from the brave and optimistic Bolshevik spirit of the early Lenin years, which was the one I looked into for my exploration into positive emotions."

The work, which he calls "cut-ups," are in an artistic continuum, from Dada to the constructivists to the modern hip-hop culture, based on recycling beats and pieces and reshaping them to realize a brand-new artistic product.

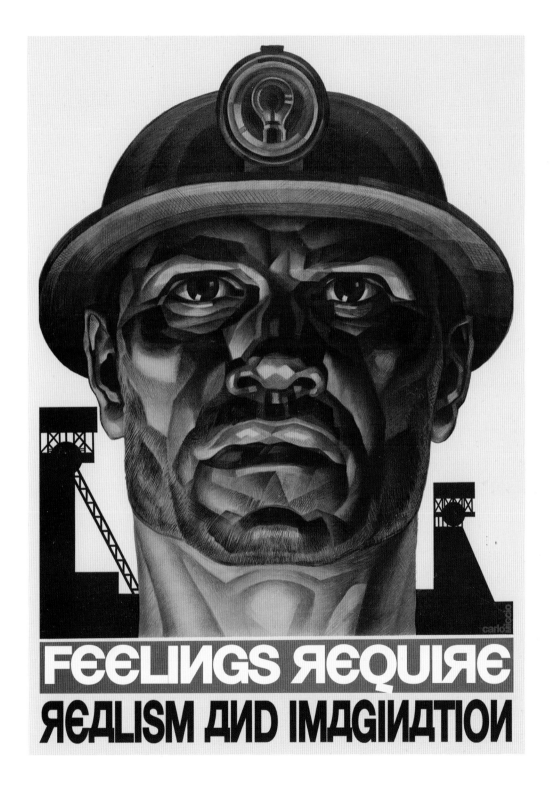

FOR FUN:

Mount the finished posters on placards and get your friends to carry them, as though in a demonstration. Or distribute them as downloads through a website.

Design a chair that is symbolically based on a famous person using styles that express his or her period of time.

STYLES: **ART DECO, VERNACULAR**

EXERCISE STEPS:

1. Decide on a subject to study.

2. Read about the life of your subject, making note of the most identifiable characteristics or quirks.

3. Determine what period your subject most represents and find a graphic style or trope to highlight that.

4. Find a chair (preferably a raw wood chair) that you will use.

5. Sketch out ideas that combine style and characteristics.

6. Make a 3-D or 2-D model before attacking the chair.

7. When confident with your idea and ability to make it concrete, go to it.

TITLE: *Assembly Required*
DESIGNERS: Justin Colt (Andy Warhol), Jinsook Bae (Adolf Hitler), Jennifer Lee (Pablo Picasso), Jung Min Kim (Jackson Pollock), Maryam Seifi (Freddie Mercury), Miao Zhao (John Lennon), Lizzy Showman (Tiger Woods), Jenny Rozbruch (Albert Einstein), Cecil Mariani (Frank Lloyd Wright), Thai Truong (Salvador Dali), Kathleen Fitzgerald (Elvis Presley), and Samia Kallidis (Alexander McQueen)

Andy Warhol Chair by Justin Colt

Students in Kevin O'Callaghan's three-dimensional illustration class, in the MFA Design/Designer as Author + Entrepreneur program at SVA, transform existing 3-D objects, including bicycles, gumball machines, pushcarts, and guitars, into artifacts that tell stories or convey messages of social, cultural, and political importance. Students adopt the style of the individual or thing being interpreted, ranging from vernacular to formalist approaches. For *Assembly Required,* the theme involved depicting famous and infamous people as children (through chairs), including Amy Winehouse, Charlie Chaplin, Andy Warhol, Adolf Hitler, Albert Einstein, Alexander McQueen, Salvador Dali, and more.

Each student began with a standard wooden IKEA chair and then cut, carved, painted, and demolished it to reflect the subject. They used a variety of graphic styles, including punk, streamline, goth, cubist, and more. The audience was challenged guessing which chair belonged to whom by virtue of the concept and style of the chair.

Adolf Hitler Chair by Jinsook Bae

Pablo Picasso Chair by Jennifer Lee

Jackson Pollock Chair by Jung Min Kim

Freddie Mercury Chair by Maryam Seifi

John Lennon Chair by Miao Zhao

Tiger Woods Chair by Lizzy Showman

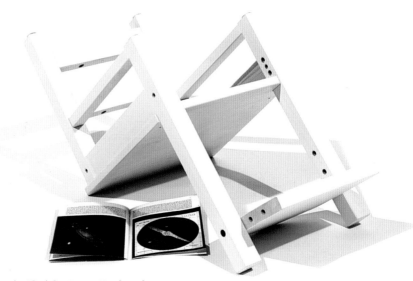

Albert Einstein Chair by Jenny Rozbruch

PLAYFUL TIP:

This requires cutting tools, hammers, nails, and other hardware. Do not work on this in your living room.

1. Think of the exercise as a small sculpture.

2. Use recyclable materials.

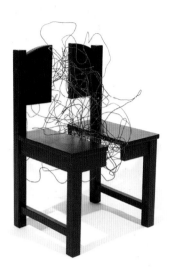

Salvador Dali Chair by Thai Truong

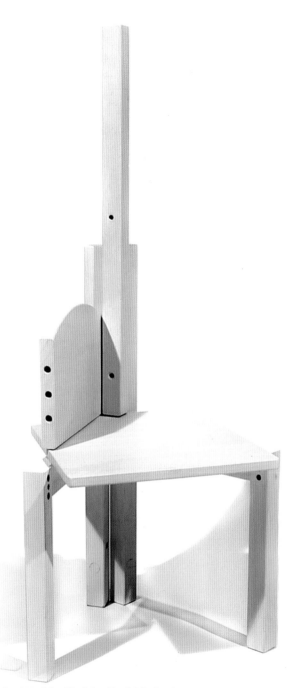

Elvis Chair by
Kathleen Fitzgerald

Frank Lloyd Wright Chair by Cecil Mariani

Alexander McQueen Chair
by Samia Kallidis

Express a personal voice in a public space.

STYLE: **VICTORIAN**

WARNING:

Public space is indeed public and governed by statutes and laws.

1. Do not trespass.
2. Look for a sponsor.
3. Make certain you have necessary permit.
4. In the case of "guerilla" posting . . . be careful.

EXERCISE STEPS:

1. Determine where this space will be (i.e., wall, bench, sidewalk, lamppost).
2. Find materials that will work well in the space you've selected.
3. Remember this is larger than your average computer screen. Your sketches should be to scale. But make various options.
4. Identify the type, ornament, and/or image you prefer.
5. Create a finished piece in your studio and physically apply it to your selected surface or paint, draw, or build your design on location.
6. Make certain to take the most advantage of the space you have selected in terms of visibility, angle, and height.

TITLE: *Authenticity Is a Popular Facade*
DESIGNER: Timothy Cohan

Timothy Cohan challenged himself by creating a large faux ghost sign on the side of a building. His phrase "Authenticity is a Popular Facade," influenced by Stefan Sagmeister's "Things I've learned in my life so far," sounds somewhat sardonic right from the start. "Applying it to a wall in a manner that looks as if it has been there for decades complements and strengthens the statement," he says about the irony of faux authenticity.

The style Cohan selected, hand painted Victorian-style lettering from New York's late nineteenth to early twentieth century, adds to the irony. This is authentic looking, but far from real. Nonetheless, the verisimilitude of the rendering makes the passerby do a double take to check its authenticity.

AUTHENTICITY
is a popular
FAÇADE

DISTINCTION

OUR   CRANKCASE
                       FLUSHED
        SYSTEM

Create a vintage typographic identity for a regional restaurant.

STYLES: **VICTORIAN, WESTERN**

EXERCISE STEPS:

1. Select a place where you would open a restaurant. (For the sake of the exercise select one where the Victorian style would be appropriate.)

2. Purchase interior design software or tools on the Web.

3. Do a digital or hand-drawn "flat plan" of the ideal interior and exterior space.

4. Design and organize the space according to where furniture and graphics will be situated.

5. Design your logo, wall signs, menus, and other graphics in the style that will define your restaurant.

6. If possible, use 3-D software to give a 360-degree view of your space.

Glossary: Flat plans are schematics or guides often created on AutoCAD by architectural draftspersons to show the interior layout of a structure. These can be done by hand or computer. There are many computer programs that provide dimensional flat plans that approximate the exact look of a space in dimension.

TITLE: Abi-Haus
DESIGNERS: Jeff Rogers and Dana Tanamachi

Graphic designer Ryan Freer decided to fulfill a dream to open his own restaurant in Abilene, Texas, and he recruited his friend Jeff Rogers to

help design the graphics. "He told me about the project early in 2012, and we started dreaming about the possibility of decking the whole place out in typographic murals," says Rogers, who asked his friend, lettering artist Dana Tanamachi, to collaborate on the lettering. Freer sought to capture a "New York City flair" mixed with a Texas flavor. "We knew we didn't want to use overly western type styles but wanted to create an eclectic visual atmosphere that combined all three of our personal styles," he says. "New York sign type and western wood type." The result was a mash-up of styles that contributed to an energetic dining atmosphere for the people of Abilene to enjoy.

GLOSSARY:

Flat plans are schematics or guides often created on AutoCAD by architectural draftspersons to show the interior layout of a structure. These can be done by hand or computer. There are many computer programs that provide dimensional flat plans that approximate the exact look of a space in dimension.

PLAYING WITH
ATTITUDE

Attitude can be mistaken for voice, but they are not the same. The latter is the personal signature of the maker; the former is the frame of a message. These distinctions may seem obtuse, but in fact this is where style is most profound. Selecting a style that underscores an attitude is essential in communicating a message without ambiguity. Attitude can be humor and wit (i.e., parody) or seriousness (pastiche). It can be demonstrative or subtle. Not every design has attitude, but when you see it you know it.

Transform a digital idea into an analog outcome.

STYLES: **ARTS AND CRAFTS, ART NOUVEAU**

EXERCISE STEPS:

1. Forget the computer for a moment. Reacquaint yourself with physical materials.

2. Read about the style of steampunk in *The Art of Steampunk: Extraordinary Devices and Ingenious Contraptions from the Leading Artists of the Steampunk Movement.*

3. Do not use the computer. Draw everything with a pencil.

4. Select graphic elements that suggest the nineteenth century.

5. Construct a prototype of an idea or contraption that might ordinarily be digital (like a small video playback or other small-screen device).

6. Find the analog corollary for it.

7. Make it.

TITLE: *Elegance, Introspection, and Sometimes Zombies*
DESIGNER: Timothy Cohan

For a class on self-promotion at the MFA Design/Designer as Author + Entrepreneur, Timothy Cohan designed a "biographical" project for a fellow student that expressed that student's visual personality. The assignment demanded a stylistic and conceptual response based on his subject's passion for collecting hundreds of pictures of all kinds on her Tumblr feed. To capture her "voice," he employed arts and crafts as well as art nouveau styling and a physical container. Cohan converted 150 of her digital images into this physical artifact—what he calls an "analog Tumblr"—made with a laser-cut design from an exotic wood known as Purple Heart. "The flowing gestures of the patterns and glass knobs with oil-rubbed bronze trim create a timeless elegance through form and materiality," he says.

TIP:

You may need to find a workshop that has an array of manual tools. And don't forget to wear protective glasses.

№18

Evoke 1920s decorative style with twenty-first-century attitude.

STYLES: **MODERNE, ART DECO**

EXERCISE STEPS:

1. Using historical influences, create a personal visual style.

2. Copy this influential work exactly as you see it.

3. Reinterpret this influential work by altering the type and image.

4. Eliminate any trace of the original work and see what remains.

5. Now, use this "style" to create your own work.

TITLES: *Advance Base; Woods Emperor X ; Chris Cohen*
DESIGNER: Sergio Membrillas

Sergio Membrillas has forged his personal style from what he refers to as "the very classic style of some modernist's posters." He refers to the French advertising placards by A.M. Cassandre, Paul Colin, and Jean Carlu, among others from the 1920s and 1930s, where an illustration "captures all your attention and works as a true claim, so the information lines work in a secondary level," he says about an approach and style generally known as moderne, modernistic, and art deco. The result is a hybrid that involves airbrush, distortion, and abstraction. While he retains a vintage accent, the overall aesthetic is not period-specific.

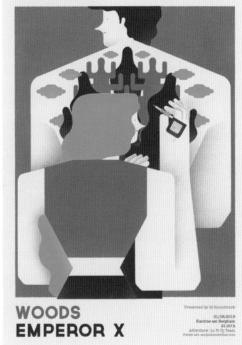

The great poster designer Lucian Bernhard was said to have developed his minimal sachplakat (object poster) style after taking an overly ornate art nouveau image and painting over all but its most essential image.

Design posters that convey graphic commentary on issues of importance for you and society.

STYLES: **EXPRESSIONISM, SURREALISM**

EXERCISE STEPS:

1. Conceive ideas that critique current views using a simple, straightforward symbolic vocabulary.

2. Make the concepts memorable through central images that speak without the need for words.

3. Employ surrealism, symbolism, and expressionism or combinations of all as a means of focusing the viewer on the idea, not the picture.

4. Print the commentaries as posters or flyers.

5. Determine whether or not people understand your message.

TITLE: Posters

DESIGNER: Mohammad Sharaf

Mohammad Sharaf is influenced by propaganda in general. In addition, he applies aspects from social realism and constructivism. "In all of my posters, I always apply a visual pun," he says. But there is more to making the imagery than stylistic exercises. "I always illustrate objects in the middle of the poster," he adds. "All my posters are printed on craft paper." In terms of content, he always tackles serious issues, but executes them in a funny way that makes them more acceptable to the public. "I leave space for the audience personal interpretation as well."

The posters here are:
1. *Censorship*
2. *Happy Woman Day*
3. *Steak of Kuwait*
4. *Saudi Women*

№ 20

Make a visual pun from a well-known logo, word mark, or trademark.

STYLES: **MODERNISM, VERNACULAR**

EXERCISE STEPS:

1. Select a mark that will be recognizable.

2. Sketch a few ideas that transform one or more marks into a message for something else.

3. Render your copy as accurately as possible. (If it is not precise, it will not have the desired effect.)

4. The success of it depends on whether you evoke a second look from your audience.

TITLE: *The Hype Over Hospital Rankings*
DESIGNER: Johnny Selman

All editorial illustrations Johnny Selman does for *The New York Times Sunday Review* are done on a tight turnaround. So the design needs to telegraph an idea to the reader in seconds. "I usually rely on familiar symbols and typography to get the job done," he says. "For this design about the role of advertising and U.S. hospitals, I used the [modern] logo for the hit TV series *Mad Men* and altered it to read, 'MedMen.' I searched for hours to find the right typeface to recreate the logo to no avail, so I ended up redrawing it. I wanted to communicate two things with this: advertising and hospitals."

PLAYFUL TIP:

A visual pun is where one image or typography has two or more meanings. In the logo for Mesa Grill, the top of the word Mesa is cut off suggesting an actual mesa. In the poster for Families, the ili are turned into a father, mother, and child. Visual puns constitute a fair number of contemporary logos.

HUBWAY

Hubway is a spot-on pun on the ubiquitous sandwich shop logo. You know what it is.

TITLE: HUBWAY

DESIGNER: Kathie Alexander

HUBWAY is for a community of Green-conscience neighbors wanting to buy local and eat local—a central location to find local farmers' markets and sell or trade farm-fresh eggs or old tomato cages. "I started this assignment by Googling logos and printing logo collections," explains Kathie Alexander. "Then came the fun part. I would get inspired and (quickly) sketch my ideas. It became a game, fun and challenging, thinking of these symbols in different ways. What spoke to me about Subway's logo were the arrows and colors. *Hub* was just the perfect replacement for *Sub*. So that's how HUBWAY was born . . . a 'hub' of Green-minded people sharing, connecting, etc. Back to the computer I went and found the Green Hub Network." The colors stayed the same because Alexander saw they fit well with the pun.

Design a DVD box set for a recent action film using type that represents the plot and time period of the movie.

STYLE: **COMIC BOOK**

EXERCISE STEPS:

1. Select an action or comic book–derived film that lends itself to being interpreted through a period or genre style (do not use illustrations—type only).

2. Specify appropriate typefaces as a pastiche of the period.

3. Challenge yourself by embellishing on the typeface(s); make the type say "Action!"

4. Apply your design to the DVDs and other ancillary material.

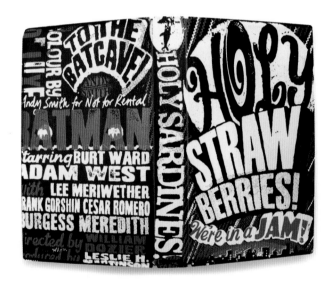

TITLE: *Holy Strawberries*
DESIGNER: Andy Smith

This piece was created for an exhibition on the theme of film imagery organized by a design company called The Church of London. Each participant had to pick a film and then design a VHS box sleeve. The title of the film could not be on the front or spine but had to be on the back of the box. Each design was then slipped in to a VHS box sleeve that was displayed on racks like an old-style video shop. "I picked the '60s Batman film for my design," says Andy Smith, who screen printed his comic lettering onto the box "to give it a really tactile feel and make the whole object the work." He wanted his piece to have a bold comic book style, "so I filled it full bleed with loud type for added chaos," he says. "The front hints at the bat signal in the sky and the back at the way blockbuster film credits are often displayed in a solid grid with no space for calm. There's also a nod to the famous POW WHACK graphics that were used in fight scenes in the early Batman series."

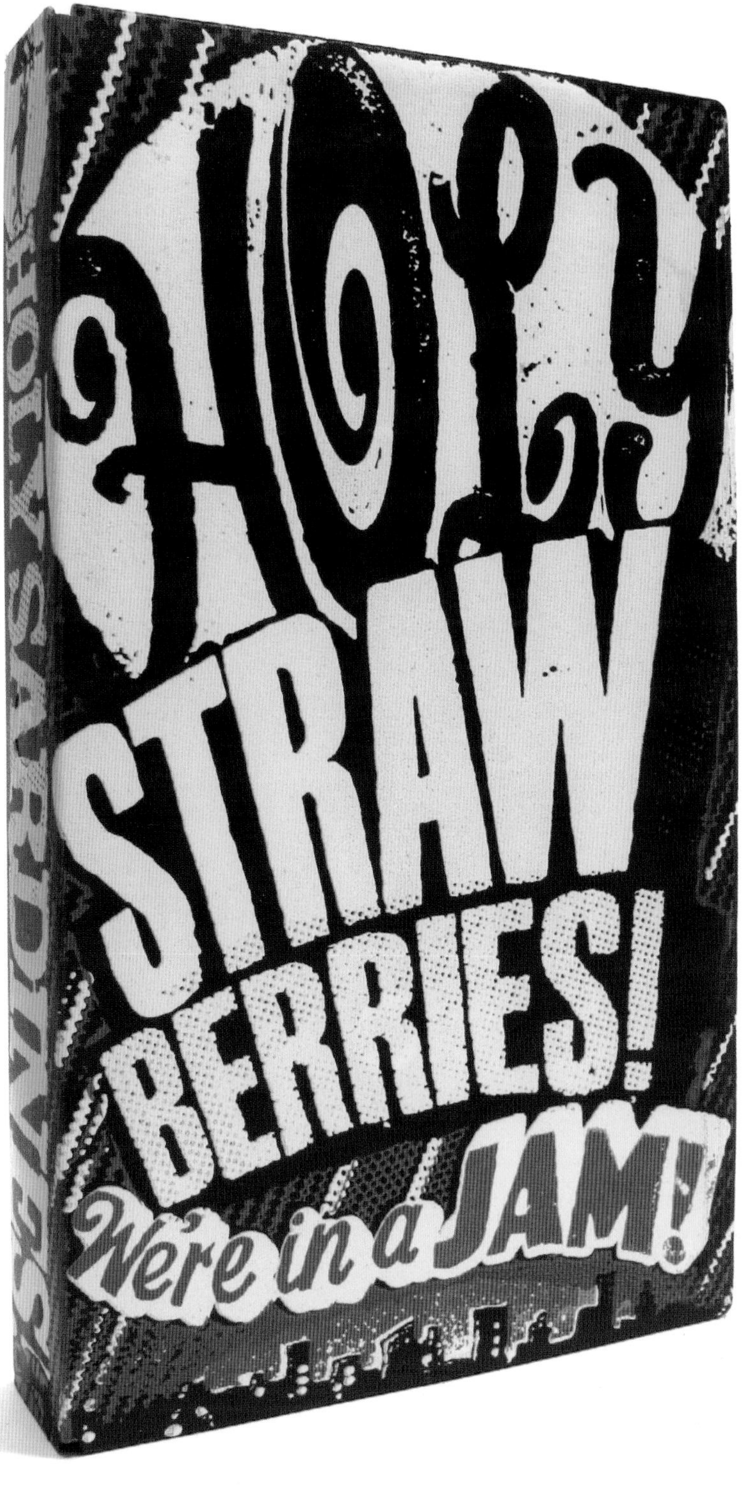
Holy
STRAW
BERRIES!
We're in a JAM!

№ 22

Create distinctive signs that you can use to sell produce in a grocery store, farmers' market, or vegetable stand.

STYLE: **VERNACULAR SIGNAGE**

EXERCISE STEPS:

1. Visit your local store or farmers' market and take notice of the signs used to sell or announce.

2. Sketch out a market of your own, filling it with various vendors, all needing signs.

3. Using existing type or custom lettering, design signs that humorously market your product.

4. The signs should be on wood, cardboard, or any surface that can be cut out.

5. Cut out your sign so it is dimensional.

TITLE: Toast Festival Signs
DESIGNER: Andy Smith

These signs, screen printed onto a plywood panel, were produced for Toast in London, a festival for food writers, restaurateurs, and chefs. They recall the style of handmade (and sometimes ad hoc) wooden signs common to roadside vegetable stands. "I wanted them to be instructional but also playful," says Andy Smith, "so I softened the type by letting it curve around the shape it sits in and tried to reflect the words in the fonts used. For instance, *Spill* has a liquid/steam feel, and *Your greens* suggest plant tendrils." He used just a few colors to give them the feel of hand-painted enamel signs. "The most important thing is that they should be fun."

NOTE:

Graphic design began in the nineteenth century in large part as a sign maker's trade. Knowing how to render precise letterforms was the most important skill that could be taught.

23

Parody any well-known rock-and-roll poster from the '60s to promote a contemporary musician.

STYLE: **PSYCHEDELIC**

EXERCISE STEPS:

1. Copy all the elements that make the original memorable.

2. Make certain that what you are parodying fits into the composition of the original.

3. Do a sketch or two of your ideas.

4. Create a finish that looks exactly like the original.

5. With nuance, tweak the finish so that it retains the original elements but has its own subtle character.

TITLE: Mo Meta Blues/?uestlove
DESIGNERS: Gail Anderson and Joe Newton

The basis for this poster is obviously the famous Milton Glaser Bob Dylan poster, which itself was a combination of a silhouette by Marcel Duchamp and color taken from a Persian miniature. "The idea came from ?uestlove himself," says Gail Anderson, "but the question mark afro was our little winky addition." They initially had mixed feelings about what felt like *ripping off* such an iconic piece of graphic design history. "To ease our consciences, we added a credit on the flap—'With apologies to Milton Glaser.' Now we won't go to design hell."

Inspiration: Milton Glaser, 1966.

THE WORLD ACCORDING TO ?UESTLOVE

AHMIR "?UESTLOVE" THOMPSON
& BEN GREENMAN

MO'
META
BLUES

WARNING:

Parody succeeds when the audience knows the original work, enabling them to be in on the joke. But a good parody should not simply mimic the original—it must "say" something new and insightful.

24

Use familiar yet novel graphics to shout out a new food product.

STYLE: **VERNACULAR**

EXERCISE STEPS:

1. Decide on a product that has mass appeal.

2. Give it a clever name.

3. Select a vernacular or retro design approach.

4. Make a trademark or trade character.

5. Design it simply (avoid flourish) yet distinctively.

TITLE: Slap Fat BrewBQ Sauce
DESIGNER: Ryan Feerer

Ryan Feerer launched his own product, Slap Fat BrewBQ Sauce, two years ago with Chad Zellner, as a way to "escape from our day-to-day responsibilities," he says. "Our intention with the stylized visuals was to have a familiar aesthetic with a contemporary twist in hopes to create a timeless label." In other words, there had to be a vernacular sensibility informed by existing brands in the genre, while at the same time a sophisticated design aesthetic. "When walking through the supermarket aisles, I noticed that all of the BBQ sauce labels were too complex and because of that, none of them stood out," Feerer explains. The Slap Fat approach needed to be simpler in order to shine among its competitors. "The combination of simple type, a tight design system that suggests stripped-down modernist style, and carefully crafted icons helps capture the simplicity, familiarity, and quirky rawness needed to bring a smile to the passerby's face."

PLAYFUL TIP:

Before starting this exercise, do some research online or in markets to see how similar products have been designed. Then do something entirely different.

1. Learn the legal restrictions regarding food packaging.

2. Include all the necessary food facts, warnings, and ingredients.

SLAPFAT BREWBQ SAUCES™

ABI TEXAS — DEVIL — NET WT 18oz

SATAN'S SAUCE
SPICY & HOT & REAL GOOD

habenero, sugar, salt, pepper, red pepper flakes, beer, vinegar, ground mustard, worcestershire, soy sauce, tomato, ketchup, molasses, smoke, chili powder, mustard, brown sugar

SLAPFAT BREWBQ SAUCES™

ABI TEXAS — DEVIL — NET WT 18oz

SPICY MUSTARD
TANGY, TASTY, AND PERFECT

mustard, jalepeño, balsamic, sugar, worcestershire, butter, pepper, salt, ground mustard, hot sauce, smoke, beer, chili powder, cumin, garlic salt, onion powder

SLAPFAT BREWBQ SAUCES™

ABI TEXAS — DEVIL — NET WT 18oz

SPICY VINEGAR
SHARP AND TANGY YUM

sugar, salt, black pepper, red pepper flakes, beer, distilled white & cider vinegar, ground mustard, worcestershire, soy sauce, tomato paste, ketchup, molasses

SLAPFAT BREWBQ SAUCES™

ABI TEXAS — DEVIL — NET WT 18oz

SLAPFAT ORIG.
FAMILIAR & DARN GOOD

sugar, salt, pepper, red pepper flakes, beer, cider vinegar, ground mustard, worcestershire, soy sauce, tomato paste, ketchup, molasses, tomato sauce

№25

Find a palatable way to express extreme violence using Saul Bass expressionism.

STYLE: **EXPRESSIONISM**

EXERCISE STEPS:

1. Become familiar with three genres: horror films, German expressionism, and Saul Bass's film titles.

2. Select three or more horror movies to illustrate as posters.

3. Sketch out variations on your themes.

4. Select the most startling and effective.

5. Render in any medium in color and black and white.

TITLE: *Living Dead Series*
DESIGNER: Julius Reyes

"How far can I push blood and gore without horrifying the audience?" asked Julius Reyes. Turning to Saul Bass's symbolic glyphs, specifically how his famous "Anatomy of a Murder" poster actually showed a dismembered body, he took his cue. "It's not horrifying because his simple style takes the shock away," Reyes reasons. Bass's style was a blend of 1920s German expressionism with a mid-century modernist accent that was abstract yet representational— symbolic and narrative. Reyes added a couple of zombie hands and a blood splatter and turned "Anatomy of a Murder" into "Night of the Living Dead." Then he repeated the process for the other two movies.

Inspiration: Saul Bass, 1959.

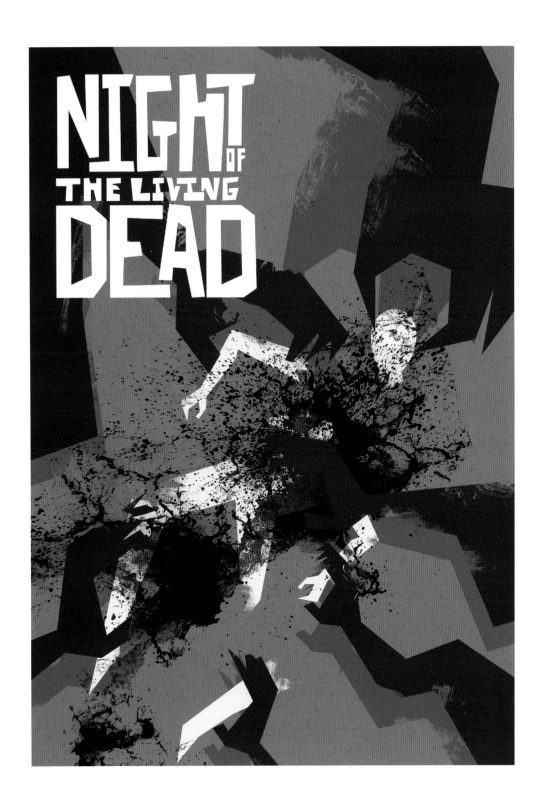

PLAYFUL TIP:

It is often more effective to suggest horror than to actually show it.

№ 26

Using only drawing, painting, and/or hand lettering, design a series of book jackets for the cannon of modern literature.

STYLES: **IMPRESSIONISM, EXPRESSIONISM, POSTMODERN**

EXERCISE STEPS:

1. Select a book or books that have well-known jackets or covers.

2. Develop a concept that illustrates the essence of the plot. This can be an illustration with lettering or illustrated lettering.

3. Determine a style or combination of styles that best represent the concept you've developed.

4. Render only by hand. (The final should look like a poster.)

TITLE: Book Covers
DESIGNER: Charlie Lewis

Charlie Lewis's plan was to break away from all the great cover designs these modern classics had in the past, "to create something fresh and interesting, whilst staying true to the source material," he explains. The styles of these covers do vary somewhat, but at the heart of all of them is a handcrafted feel that is essential to his work. Because the majority of Lewis's process occurs digitally, it is important for the different elements of the image to start off as traditional marks on paper. "These marks, shapes, and textures are manipulated digitally and brought together forming a kind of collage to create the final image, allowing me to have bold, vibrant work with a noticeably human touch."

PLAYFUL TIP:

This exercise allows you freedom to mix styles but also stay true to the content of the material.

1. Do not simply illustrate a passage from the book.

2. Do not copy or imitate any type or image from the original book.

3. Be abstract if you like, but not obscure.

Use delftware pottery designs as a narrative element.

STYLE: **DELFTWARE**

EXERCISE STEPS:

1. Study the history of delftware.

2. Determine a conceptual reason for applying it.

3. Sketch various patterns to feel comfortable copying the form.

4. Conceive a visual idea in which delft works best.

5. Copy the style onto your idea.

TITLE: *Re-Elect George Washington*
DESIGNER: Kathleen Fitzgerald
(Collaboration with Lauren Kolesinskas)

For a conceptual election-year exhibition titled *Re-Elect* at the School of Visual Arts, participants were required to visually repackage former American presidents as though they were running for office today. Kathleen Fitzgerald selected George Washington, which suggested using a Colonial American style, notably the famous delftware pottery designs ubiquitous in the colonies in the eighteenth century.

At a quick glance, the wallpaper created for this installation piece is a seemingly classic representation of iconic delft porcelain found in English homes, but, upon closer look, the distorted and mildly cartoonish visuals of the Battle of Yorktown "help to modernize the piece and engage the viewers," she says about the motif used on various modern electoral souvenirs, coffee cups, notebooks, and so on. "I love to use somewhat shocking visuals in subtle ways to encourage my audiences to think and to be observant." Tweaking such a familiar stylistic motif forces a double take, and then comes the aha realization that something more than the quotation of history is in play.

NOTE:

Avoid anachronisms. Designers are occasionally asked to parody certain vintage and contemporary fashions. Before you do, learn which of these is most appropriate for your design problem.

SEQUITUR

CODE

DAY 1

DAY 2

PLAYING WITH

SIMPLICITY + COMPLEXITY

These are the two poles of graphic design. Some styles are simple or minimal, others are complex or maximal. Both are valid. There is little in between. You cannot be a little simple or a tad complex. Historical styles fluctuate between the poles. Art nouveau is by definition overwrought, modernism is reductive. It is useful to experiment with both. See how well complexity works for you. Try minimalism as a method, too. Start large and reduce to small. Design is a wonderful platform on which to play—and to add and subtract.

Use silk screen or letterpress to reproduce
a series of inspirational signs and posters
with bold wood type or metal lettering.

STYLES: **LETTERPRESS, VERNACULAR**

EXERCISE STEPS:

1. Locate a commercial or school print shop that can
   provide instruction in vintage printing techniques.

2. Collect samples from libraries or flea markets of
   bold typographies.

3. Invent a reason for creating these posters.

4. Write slogans and aphorisms that may inspire
   or caution.

5. Print them in one or more colors.

6. Post around home, schools, or the neighborhood.

TITLE: Is This a Technology Company?
DESIGNER: Ben Barry

Ben Barry is the founder of Analog Research Laboratory at Facebook, where he established a screen-printing studio to print graphically simple one-color, big type posters. "I didn't specifically set out to mimic or copy any particular piece or style," he admits. But he was influenced by a 1922 antiwar poster that was simple, type only, yet radical. Following the poster's lead, Barry decided to reprint phrases/mantras he heard around the company, such as "Move Fast and Break Things," as well as things he'd written down over the years from numerous sources. "There was no official project, no approval process, I just did it. From the start, people were very curious about the posters. Some resonated, some didn't. The community questioned, altered, vandalized, and made them their own. Eventually, people found out I was behind them, and started reaching out to me with ideas of their own. I believe if we're doing our job then people feel control and ownership over their physical environment, and I believe that translates to them feeling more empowered in all the other aspects of their jobs."

MOVE FAST AND BREAK THINGS

THIS POSTER BROUGHT TO YOU BY THE FACEBOOK ANALOG RESEARCH LABORATORY

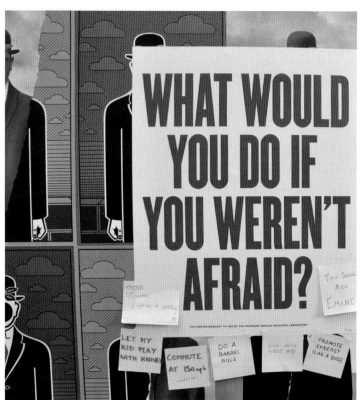

PLAYFUL TIP:

You can start your own movement or campaign just by spreading your words via your posters.

№ 29

Use airbrush to create a streamlined heroic representation on a poster for a sporting event.

STYLES: **ART DECO, STREAMLINE, SURREALISM**

EXERCISE STEPS:

1. After selecting an event, research photos of athletes to understand their muscularity.

2. Practice your airbrush rendering either manually or on the computer.

3. Compose the poster to emphasize the image against the backdrop of the typography.

4. Add whatever additional image elements are needed to underscore heroic.

TITLE: *London 2012*
DESIGNER: Paul Rogers

"I don't want to merely ape the vintage style without bringing something of my own to the image," confesses Paul Rogers. "This one toes the line and probably actually crosses it with both feet." Joseph Binder did a cover for *Gebrauchsgraphik* in 1935 that Rogers had been carrying around in his head since he first saw it, "and for some reason this seemed like the time to try to drag that image into the present day. The influence of Binder on a lot of my work is obvious and on this one I'm not sure I really brought enough new baggage to the piece. To make matters worse, I also imitated another hero of mine, McKnight Kauffer, for the London landmarks in the background. I know, I know, it's sad."

LONDON 2012

PAUL ROGERS · KILLINGTONARTS.COM

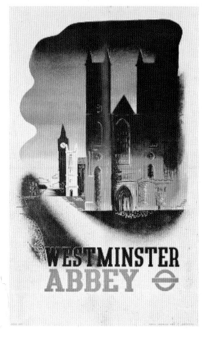

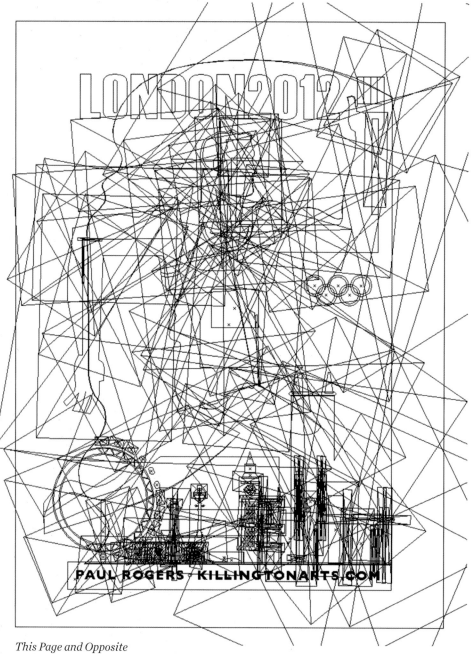

This Page and Opposite
Inspiration: E. McKnight Kauffer, 1930s.

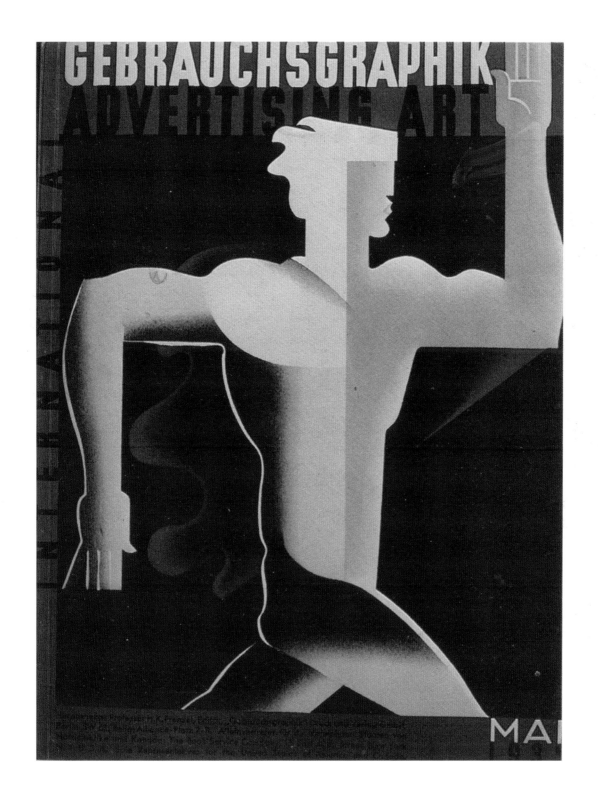

121

30

Conceive a series of recruitment posters for a college continuing education program.

STYLE: **MODERN**

EXERCISE STEPS:

1. Determine a program at your school that needs promotion.

2. Develop a campaign of three or four posters that will draw students to the program.

3. Make the posters as simple yet recognizable as possible.

4. Use only two (but any two) colors.

5. Use only sans serif type in only two weights.

TITLE: CS Poster Series for Howard University
DESIGNER: Johnny Selman

A well-known software engineer at Google was teaching two classes at Howard University when Johnny Selman was asked to create a poster series to drum up interest for the class on campus. "Robert Wong, CD at Google Creative Lab, told me that Computer Science has a marketing problem and that this is an opportunity for us to start to fix that. I wanted the poster series to be bold, colorful, and energetic. I wanted the series to tell a story about the power of code." With a set of six colors and a bold sans serif typeface he went at it. "The common denominator was the word code, and accompanying words (design, create, made, and so on) were overlaid, stretching to the edges of the posters. I think that the scale in the compositions shows that while code is the constant, the possibilities and opportunities are immense."

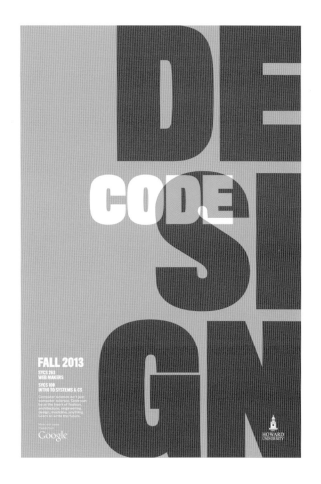

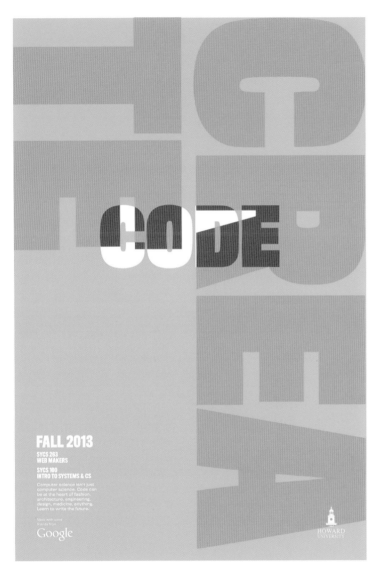

31

Create optical iterations of the letters.

STYLES: **PSYCHEDELIC, OP ART**

EXERCISE STEPS:

1. Choose a word and make a poster of each of the letters.

2. Study the 1960s styles of psychedelic and op art.

3. Locate or create vibrating and contrasting patterns.

4. The patterns will serve as camouflage for the letters.

5. Integrate the patterns and letter, which is also patterned together.

6. When complete, the letter should blend into the background so it is barely discernable.

TITLE: *Hatched*
DESIGNERS: Justin Colt, Jose Fresneda, Lizzy Showman, and Jenny Rozbruch

A blocky custom typeface was designed for the logo of *Hatched*, an exhibition of the 2013 graduates of MFA Design/Designer as Author + Entrepreneur at SVA. It was rendered in a variety of black-and-white optical iterations. The problem for the poster designer was to riff on and interpret individual letters of the title, so that it would be visible and invisible at the same time. The solution was inspired by psychedelic and op art styles, which flipped the rules around: Instead of making a poster visible from ten feet away, make it visible from only ten inches away. The letters each recede into the background. With a strong enough stare, the letter did, however, come forward through what is essentially psychedelic/op art camouflage.

EXTRA:

Do the same with black and white only and vibrating colors to see which color combinations vibrate the most.

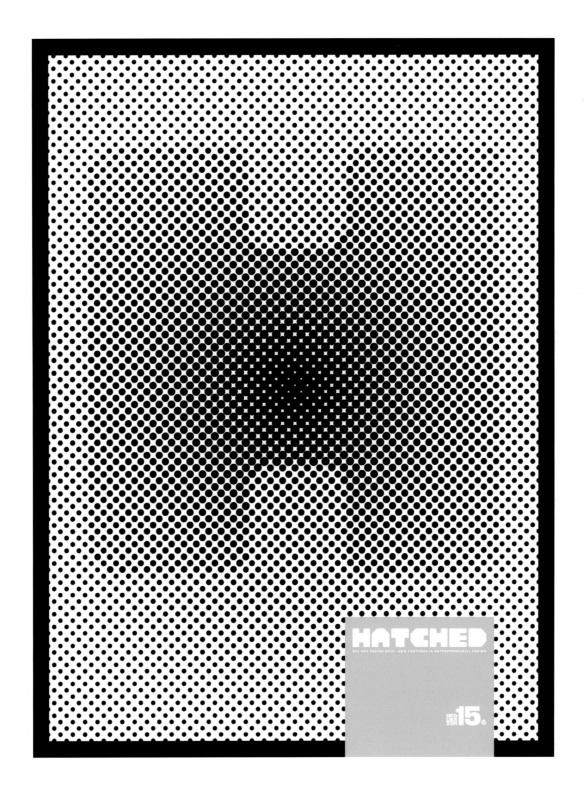

№32

Provide distinct identities for a single company's various products.

STYLES: **VICTORIAN, MODERNE, MODER**

EXERCISE STEPS:

1. Select a company (such as General Foods) that has many different product brand lines.

2. Choose four or five products.

3. Determine what you visually want to say about this group of products.

4. There must be a common visual or typographic thread.

5. Design a series of labels or packages that ties them together yet makes them totally unique.

For Fun: Make the products so they are marketed through different graphics to high- and low-end consumption.

TITLE: Liquid Shot Co.
DESIGNER: Ryan Feerer

Liquid Shot Co. specializes in quality single-use packaging or single-serve items, which as a rule is packaged for the mass consumer. For Liquid Shot Co., the approach needed to feel unique and high-end. Ryan Feerer introduced a range of vintage styles used to define each individual product. For every beverage category there is a different design system. It enables both the company and customer to feel the products are different enough—special—but when seen together, they still feel like a family. "That is a difficult task when you are designing for a wide demographic," says Feerer. The typographic choices, rooted in nineteenth- and early-twentieth-century styles, provide a sense of heritage as well as variety.

FOR FUN:

Make the products so they are
marketed through different graphics
to high- and low-end consumption.

disposable
measuring cups

for all your
food prep needs

TITLE: Messless

DESIGNER: Kathie Alexander

Messless was inspired by the Martha Stewart line of disposable prep items for the kitchen. Kathie Alexander hopes that someday most kitchen items will be disposable and doing the dishes or loading the dishwasher will be obsolete. Borrowing a page from Martha's style guide, Alexander uses rich brown with a hint of pastel, making an otherwise vintage look very here and now.

M LE E S S S

disposable cutting boards

for all your food prep needs

Use familiar objects in unexpected ways.

STYLE: **VERNACULAR**

EXERCISE STEPS:

1. Select your favorite everyday objects.

2. Photograph them from different angles.

3. Use the object(s) as illustration.

4. Write and design type for a title or headline of a book cover or poster.

5. Integrate the object with the typography.

TITLES: *An Early History of Fire; The Russian Transport*
DESIGNERS: RED/Stuart Rogers and Sam Eckersley

The New Group is an off-Broadway theater company that caters to a very literary audience. The 2012 season was devoted to intimate storytelling, and RED utilized detailed macrophotographs of familiar objects to convey that intimacy. "We've always enjoyed presenting familiar objects in unexpected ways," Stuart Rogers notes, "and this campaign was a great opportunity to do that.

Each photo came with a twist to intrigue the audience." In *The Russian Transport,* RED painted traditional Russian nesting dolls with a less-than-traditional reveal, while in *An Early History of Fire*, they montaged two photographs together to create the single flame effect. Clean typography and solid backgrounds finished the look. The typography was stylistically neutral but contemporary; the familiar objects were surprises for the viewer.

PLAYFUL TIP:

Virtually any static form can be made into an illustration.

1. Turn your object into a meaningful symbol.

2. Photograph your object in motion.

3. Add different textures to your object.

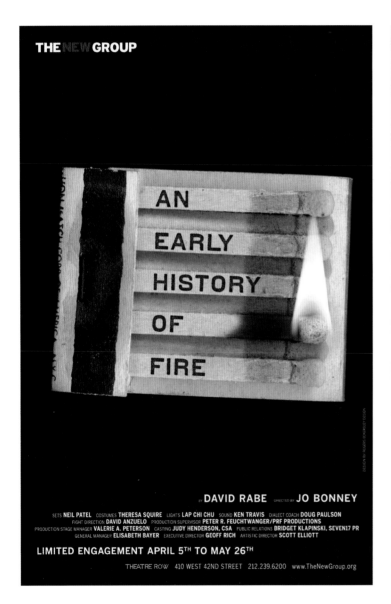

THE NEW GROUP

AN
EARLY
HISTORY
OF
FIRE

BY **DAVID RABE** DIRECTED BY **JO BONNEY**

SETS **NEIL PATEL** COSTUMES **THERESA SQUIRE** LIGHTS **LAP CHI CHU** SOUND **KEN TRAVIS** DIALECT COACH **DOUG PAULSON**
FIGHT DIRECTION **DAVID ANZUELO** PRODUCTION SUPERVISOR **PETER R. FEUCHTWANGER/PRF PRODUCTIONS**
PRODUCTION STAGE MANAGER **VALERIE A. PETERSON** CASTING **JUDY HENDERSON, CSA** PUBLIC RELATIONS **BRIDGET KLAPINSKI, SEVEN17 PR**
GENERAL MANAGER **ELISABETH BAYER** EXECUTIVE DIRECTOR **GEOFF RICH** ARTISTIC DIRECTOR **SCOTT ELLIOTT**

LIMITED ENGAGEMENT APRIL 5TH TO MAY 26TH

THEATRE ROW   410 WEST 42ND STREET   212.239.6200   www.TheNewGroup.org

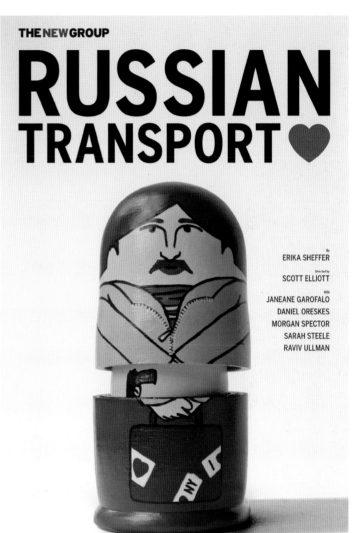

THE NEW GROUP

RUSSIAN
TRANSPORT ♥

By
ERIKA SHEFFER

Directed by
SCOTT ELLIOTT

With
JANEANE GAROFALO
DANIEL ORESKES
MORGAN SPECTOR
SARAH STEELE
RAVIV ULLMAN

STARTS JANUARY 17, 2012
THEATRE ROW   410 WEST 42ND STREET   212.239.6200   www.TheNewGroup.org

Design maps with distinct stylistic personalities.

STYLES: **CLASSICAL, VERNACULAR, ART DECO**

EXERCISE STEPS:

1. Select two or three different country or city maps. Determine a style that is appropriate for each one (art deco for Paris, classical for Rome, etc.).

2. Design a legend with the typography of the respective era.

3. Add other stylistic traits to the maps.

4. Make certain the map is readable.

TITLE: *Maps*
DESIGNER: Neil Gower

Topology is as diverse as the world is large; therefore, it is logical that maps should also be different from place to place—and from artist to artist. Neil Gower is stylistically many artists in one. His maps illustrate more than the featured locals, but a conceptual challenge: to design each using a different historical or contemporary style that bolsters the geographical area under consideration.

PLAYFUL TIP:

Illustrated and designed maps are in demand to provide information and spruce up layouts. Maps also come in all shapes and sizes. Play with them.

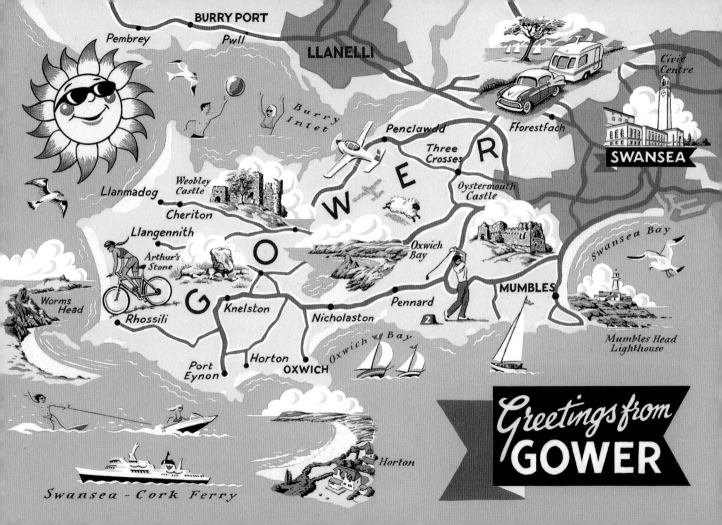

Greetings from GOWER

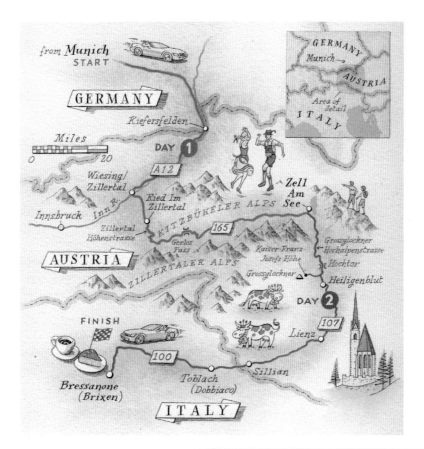

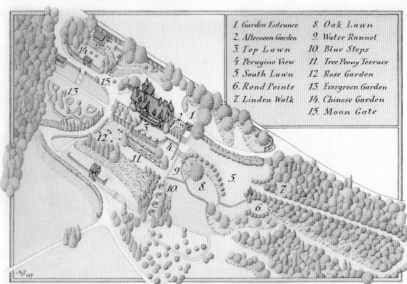

1. Garden Entrance	8. Oak Lawn
2. Afternoon Garden	9. Water Runnel
3. Top Lawn	10. Blue Steps
4. Perugino View	11. Tree Peony Terrace
5. South Lawn	12. Rose Garden
6. Rond Pointe	13. Evergreen Garden
7. Linden Walk	14. Chinese Garden
	15. Moon Gate

№35

Make what is a frequently impersonal experience into a more comfortable one through a product designed in a friendly, nostalgic package.

STYLES: **LETTERPRESS, VERNACULAR**

EXERCISE STEPS:

1. Select an experience (e.g., paying bills, seeing a doctor, applying for a permit).
2. Determine what product concept would make this experience more palatable.
3. Determine a form your product should take.
4. Select a style, write copy, and determine a format.
5. Make variations in different colors and typefaces.

TITLE: Post-Op Departure Packs
DESIGNER: Jenny Rozbruch

In light of today's often cold and impersonal hospital experience, Jenny Rozbruch created personalized "Post-Op Departure Packs" to provide patients with comfort, security, and clear information in the days after an operation. "The design is intended to hark back to the more romantic days of medicine in the 1950s—when candy stripers roamed the hospital and medical packaging was bright and friendly—and bring some of that warmth back into today's hospitals," she says. "I adapted common colors, forms, and overall styles found in vintage medical graphics to create a contemporary yet nostalgic product."

VINTAGE MEDICAL GRAPHICS

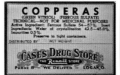

Post-Operative Instructions

Wound Care

Rx
PRESCRIPTION POUCH

#1 RULE:
If it hurts, don't do it.

DAY 1

- Rest and don't work through the
- Take pain killers when you start
- Ice continuously over bandage (lo
- Don't force muscles to stretch if t
- Elevate limb as much as possible t
- Take temperature twice a day unt in record keeper attached).
- Use supports provided (i.e. cane, crut
- Ignore any black and blue marks.
- Swelling at surgical site and beyond bandage if it feels too tight).
- Reinforce dressing with a towel if dr
- If given precautions by Dr. Roabruch.

Surgery Art

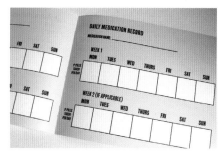

DAILY MEDICATION RECORD

MEDICATION NAME:

WEEK 1

MON	TUES	WED	THURS	FRI	SAT	SUN

WEEK 2 (IF APPLICABLE)

MON	TUES	WED	THURS	FRI	SAT	SUN

Cold Comfort

Patient Name

PLAYFUL TIP:

The goal is to identify an experience that requires instructions or other reading matter that will inform and entertain.

№36

Transform sound into visual representation of music.

STYLES: **GERMAN EXPRESSIONISM, PSYCHEDELIC**

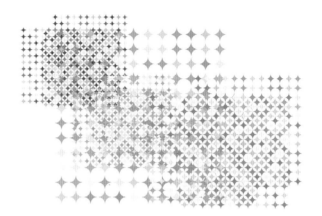

EXERCISE STEPS:

1. Select a piece of music that stimulates your visual imagination.

2. Determine what existing styles best suggest the musical range. For purposes of this exercise, try an expressionist style.

3. Use paint, ink, or woodcut as your interpretive medium.

4. Design glyphs or symbols to replace sound. Select type to complement the glyphs.

5. Compose in static or motion these glyphs to represent the flow of the music.

6. Make your "flowchart" into a poster format—and watch as people interpret it.

TITLE: Sequitur
DESIGNER: Cecil Mariani

"I have always been puzzled," says Cecil Mariani, "about how music can be visually represented in a particular style that looks like music, but not too random." Sequitur is a branding program for contemporary music based on a twelve-tone matrix of Arnold Schoenberg, the Austrian composer and painter, associated with the expressionism movement in German poetry and art.

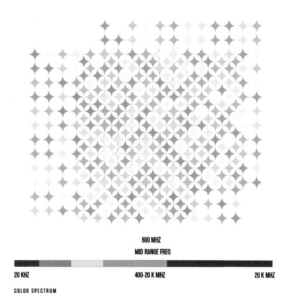

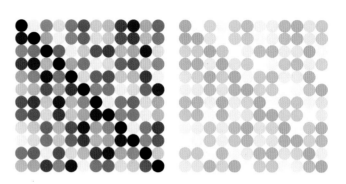

NOTE:

Although this outcome is rather abstract, your end product will be very concrete. Use the music to take your design into a space you've never been.

HAROLD MELTZER   CO-ARTISTIC
                    DIRECTOR

(917) 664-1502
HAROLDMELTZER@GMAIL.COM
WWW.SEQUITUR.ORG

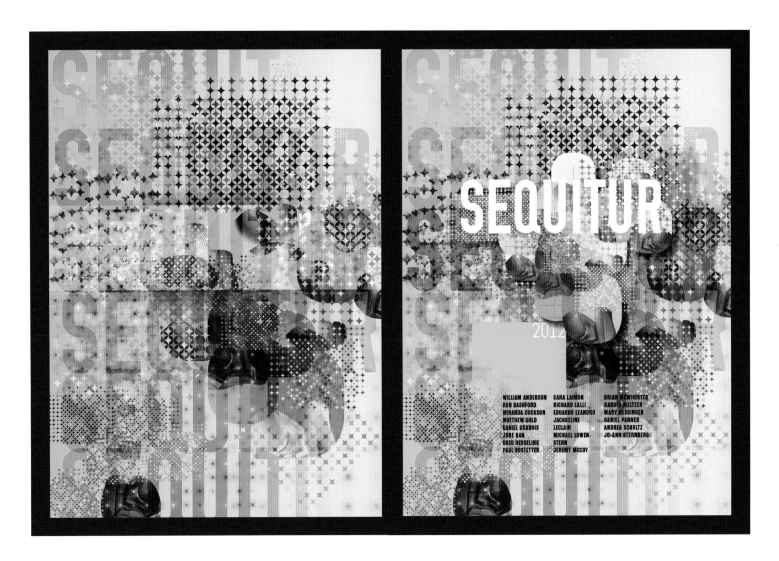

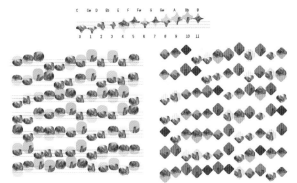

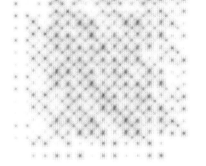

PLAYING WITH

Symbolic

TYPE

T ype is the graphic designer's language (a.k.a. lingua franca). It can be neutral or transparent, enabling the reader to parse text without interference. Or it can be boisterous, loud to grab attention. It also has symbolic power. Certain typefaces represent specific things. We see the face and reflexively think of a person, place, or thing. History provides many stylistically rich typographic examples that trigger familiarity. Playing with style enables designers to work with typefaces that may be alien to them, but nonetheless opens a realm of shorthand communications.

Create a blackletter typeface that is old and new.

STYLE: **PLAKATSTIL/SACHPLAKAT (POSTER STYLE/OBJECT POSTER)**

EXERCISE STEPS:

1. Research vintage German blackletter typefaces and posters using them. (A good history is *Blackletter: Type and National Identity* by Paul Shaw and Peter Bain [Princeton Architectural Press], and a good online source is www.linotype.com/ 2221/ blackletterfonts.html.)

2. With a pencil, trace the letterforms you find most appealing.

3. Using a font-creation tool, begin drawing these letters until you have a complete alphabet.

4. Finalize the alphabet and test its viability.

5. Apply the alphabet to a medium—book, poster, CD, and so on.

6. Give it a name.

TITLE: Dark Angel
DESIGNER: Michael Doret

Michael Doret thought it opportune to develop a typeface that is both retro and current, "a new blackletter hybrid style," he says. "None of them are specifically based on any existing Gothic/blackletter fonts. It was the one in the middle that I eventually expanded into Dark Angel." There is an influence of Lucian Bernhard (creator of sachplakat), which Doret does not deny, "but in this instance it was more subliminal and unconscious than overt . . . probably more the *spirit* of his graphic style permeating this font than anything specific."

This font is virtually Brimming Over with all kinds of Swashes, Ligatures, Alternates and Special Features!

And he seized the dragon, that ancient serpent, who is the devil and Satan, and bound him for a thousand years.

And he seized the dragon, that ancient serpent, who is the devil and Satan, and bound him for a thousand years.

Design custom lettering based on classic banknotes, deeds, or stock certificates.

STYLES: **VICTORIAN, BANKNOTE/STOCK CERTIFICATE**

EXERCISE STEPS:

1. Write headlines that you will illustrate with your lettering.

2. As reference, review the various kinds of vintage "official" certificates with engraved filigree borders.

3. Duplicate the precise method with which these engravings were made.

4. Compose your layout carefully and precisely. Faithful duplication is the key to making this succeed.

TITLES: IMA Salary Survey; *Sports Illustrated* "The 50 Greatest Sports Figures"; *Businessweek* "America's Boom"
DESIGNER: Daniel Pelavin

This design motif is ideal for illustrating financial themes, but as the *Sports Illustrated* cover evidences, anything that suggests "official" or "celebration" are good themes as well. But there is more to making custom letterforms: "The act of designing is, for me, infusing the process of communication with delight," says Daniel Pelavin. "Should the stylistic idiom reference the content and resonate with the viewer, all the better. However, my ultimate goal is the sharing of information in a way that engages, informs, and provides a pleasant journey for the eye."

PLAYFUL TIP:

You can find templates for stock certificates on the Internet. (Google "stock certificates.")

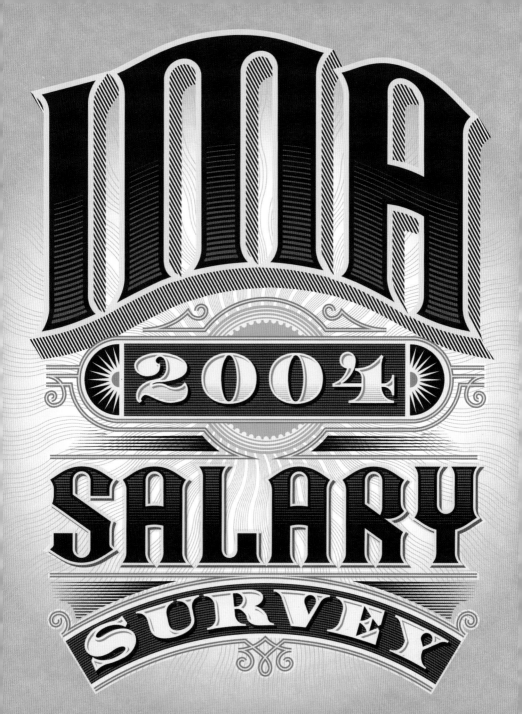

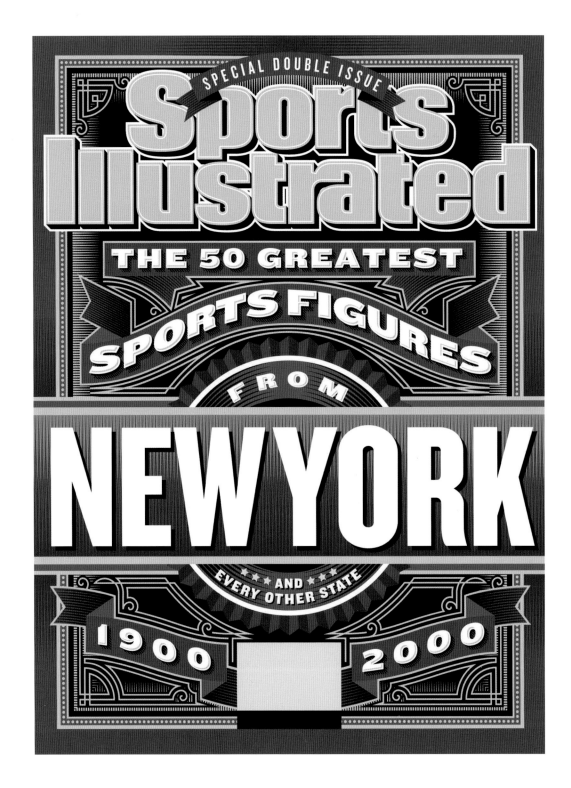

Design a typographic sign, billboard, or mural that looks both old and new.

STYLE: **VERNACULAR**

NOTE:

For maximum impact, make dimensionalized or shadowed letters. Use startling, even vibrating, colors to add luminosity to your design.

EXERCISE STEPS:

1. Familiarize yourself with different kinds of American billboards and painted signs.

2. Select and photograph an empty surface—wall, fence, hoarding. This will become your "canvas."

3. Determine your message.

4. Do sketches of your hand-lettered message.

5. Using your computer, apply layout/composition to the empty surface.

6. Paint (by hand) your final message and Photoshop it onto the empty surface to see exactly how it will fit in the environment.

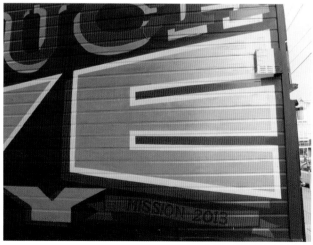

TITLE: *Love Wall*

DESIGNER: Pablo Medina

Pablo Medina was in San Francisco in the spring of 2011 as part of an artist-in-residence program at California College of the Arts. While there, he created a series of lettering paintings that used the many hand-painted signs in the Mission District as influence. One of those paintings became the blueprint for the mural. He used exterior house paint, gold spray paint, paint rollers and brushes, a chalk line, chalk, and two ladders. It was an homage to the people of the city.

Design a book cover or poster that combines different styles of lettering into one startling typographic approach.

STYLE: **1970s GLAM**

EXERCISE STEPS:

1. Select three or four type styles from different periods.
2. Match up the different letters to create disharmony among them.
3. Select elements of each style and combine them into one letter.
4. Make an alphabet out of this hybrid combo.
5. Using this alphabet, compose a typographic layout.
6. Add whatever flourishes you deem useful.

TITLE: *The Rolling Stones 50 Licks*
DESIGNERS: Gail Anderson and Joe Newton

Gail Anderson and Joe Newton wanted to do a '70s glam cover, riffing off the Studio 54 disco decadence of the era. "But we still wanted it to include some contemporary conceits, like the slightly weathered background," Anderson explains. "The typeface is Strand Midnite, by Device. The initial cover had no photo until the editor requested one, but we came around to liking it that way pretty quickly. We are nothing if not flexible."

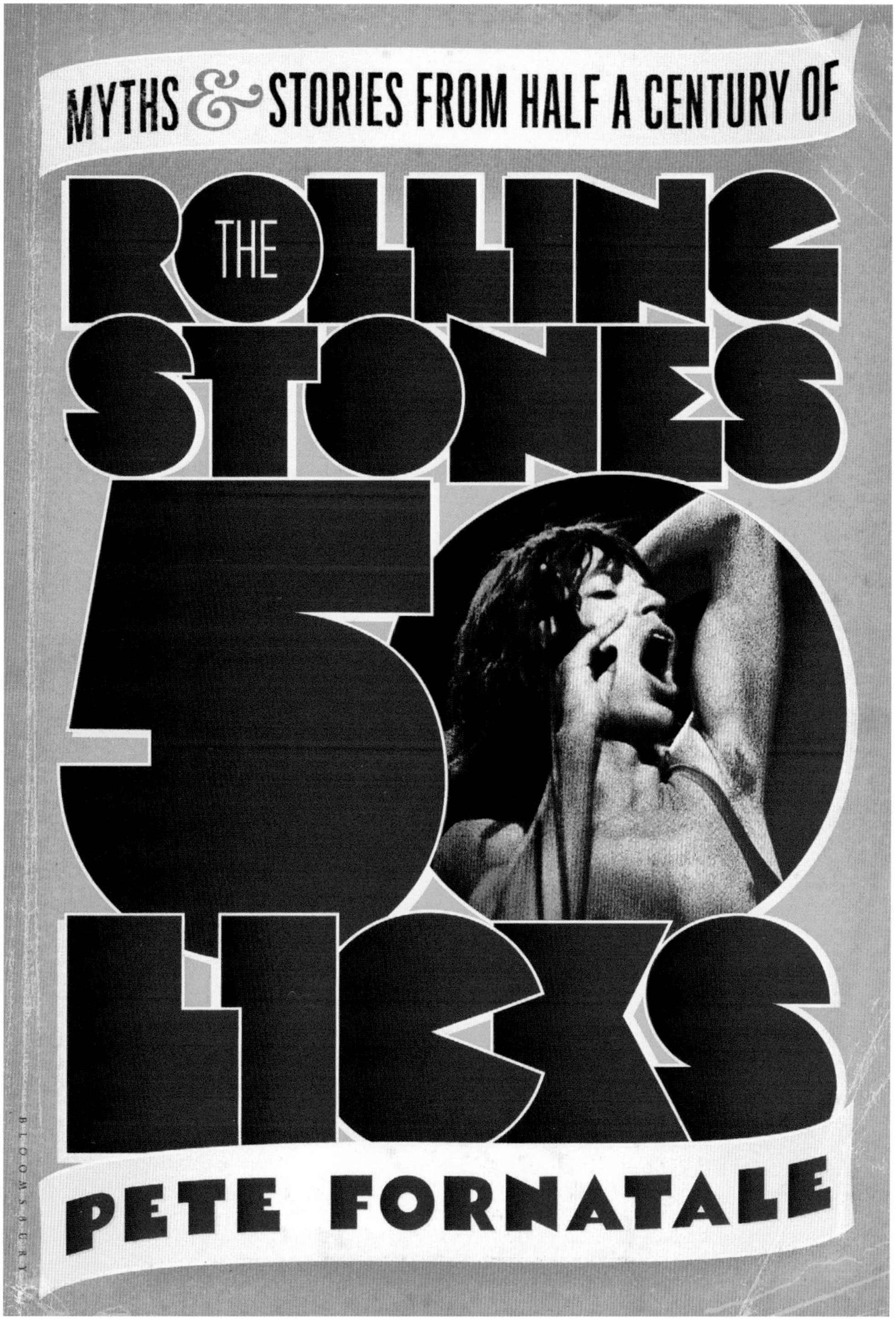

MYTHS & STORIES FROM HALF A CENTURY OF

THE ROLLING STONES

50 LICKS

PETE FORNATALE

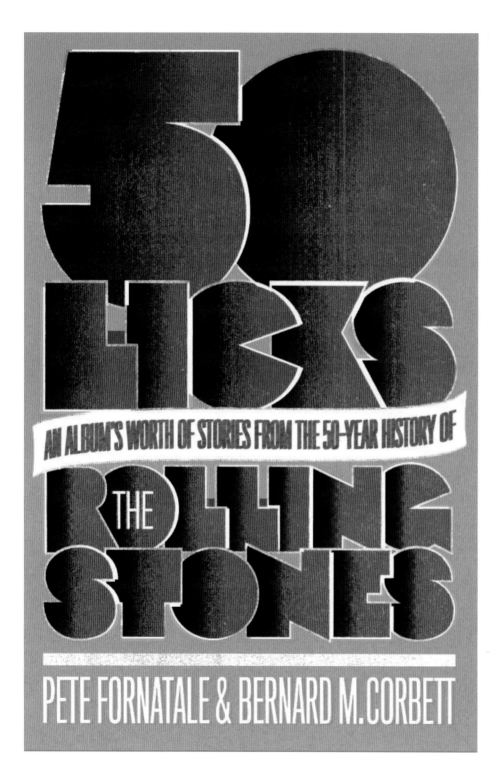

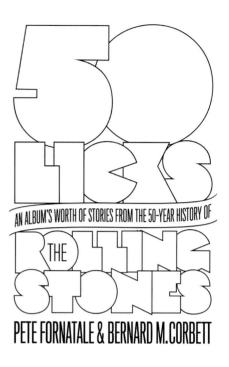

PLAYFUL TIP:

The object of this exercise is to see how many unique variations can be made by three or more lettering/type styles. Don't be afraid to mix as many as you can.

AN ALBUM'S WORTH OF STORIES FROM THE 50-YEAR HISTORY OF

THE ROLLING STONES

50 LICKS

PETE FORNATALE & BERNARD M. CORBETT

Make words into signs and signs into words.

STYLE: **THEATER MARQUEE VERNACULAR**

EXERCISE STEPS:

1. Find pictures of vintage theater marquees from movie palaces, Broadway, or clubs.

2. Make exact copies of the marquees you find. You will want to use different marquees as the basis for your words.

3. Paint or draw these signs; avoid using the computer.

4. Sketch words or sentences out of three or more different signs.

5. Compose them in a distinct readable arrangement.

TITLE: *No One Will Ever Know, et al…*
DESIGNER: Jeff Rogers

Drawing type by hand offers Jeff Rogers flexibility. He can use a large variety of type styles in a single piece. Of the letterforms he enjoys most, vintage theater marquee lights are at the top of the list. Instead of hunting for fonts, he just draws the letters as he imagines them. He spent several years in New York City designing Broadway show posters and has been enamored with the old lightbulb-and-neon-sign style of type ever since. "It was a total cliché to use this influence in the context of Broadway theater," he says, "but I've found that when put into other contexts, the result is pretty interesting." He also likes the juxtaposition of mundane words as huge neon signs. "When I am making type into a sign, I almost feel like I am the sign maker," he says.

PLAYFUL TIP:

Make them look old, paint them on board, cover with glaze, or add highlights for dimensionality.

42

Use movie house vernacular as a title for a theatrical performance.

STYLE: **MOVIE MARQUEE VERNACULAR**

EXERCISE STEPS:

1. See how many different classic movie theater marquees you can find.

2. Collect photographs for reference.

3. Either scan or trace the marquees.

4. Make letters from the classic signs. You might also find actual letters to use.

5. Create a design composition, either digitally or by hand, that feels as though the letters were photographed on a real marquee.

TITLE: *The Flick*

DESIGNERS: RED/Stuart Rogers and Sam Eckersley

The Flick is a salute to the dying culture of 35 mm film, with the entire play set in a crumbling old movie theater. RED was immediately inspired by a photograph of a theater with an old film marquee (before it was replaced by a digital sign). "When our original photographic approach didn't feel gritty enough, designer Jamus Marquette changed it to an illustration," explains Sam Eckersley. Based on classic theater signage and fonts, the sign was first designed in Illustrator and then photocopied about twenty times to get this great texture that speaks perfectly to the tone of the play.

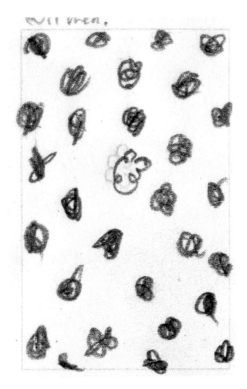

THE FLICK

BY ANNIE BAKER

DIRECTED BY SAM GOLD

PLAYWRIGHTS HORIZONS

43

Reinterpret classic circus poster lettering.

STYLE: **AMERICAN CIRCUS POSTER VERNACULAR**

EXERCISE STEPS:

1. Review the circus type samples shown here and found at www.1001fonts.com/circus+poster-fonts.html.
2. Combine different typefaces to find the right compositional balance.
3. Use free fonts from the Web or printed sources.
4. Make your own versions of these letters.
5. Combine them to make a message.

TITLE: *Jersey Strong*
DESIGNER: Jeff Rogers

Hand-painted lettering allows Jeff Rogers to interpret, modify, and even fudge those vintage and vernacular original typefaces from which he draws inspiration, making them more contemporary and fun. "For this mural [for a gym in New Jersey], I wanted to try and use the influence and energy of vintage circus posters," he explains. The type flips and flops all over the place, becomes a set of dumbbells, and wraps itself around the arms of the strong man, who has been cropped off the bottom. A feeling of fun and whimsy is induced by using a variety of type styles, bright colors, banners, and playful imagery. The look of a circus poster is apparent to all who ever attended a performance and recognize the inspiration, but the result is decidedly a personalized application of the form.

PLAYFUL TIP:

To show the versatility of this style, design your letters in an array of different colors.

....

1. Do everything monochromatic.
2. Add color to the interior of letters.
3. Make drop shadows in carnival colors.
4. (If you can, read *The Circus 1870s–1950s* by Linda Granfield, Dominique Jando, Fred Dahlinger, and Noel Daniel [Taschen] to determine your design direction.)

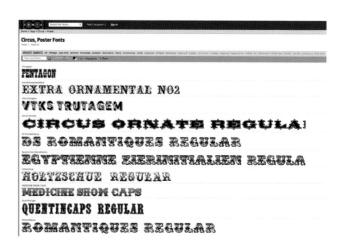

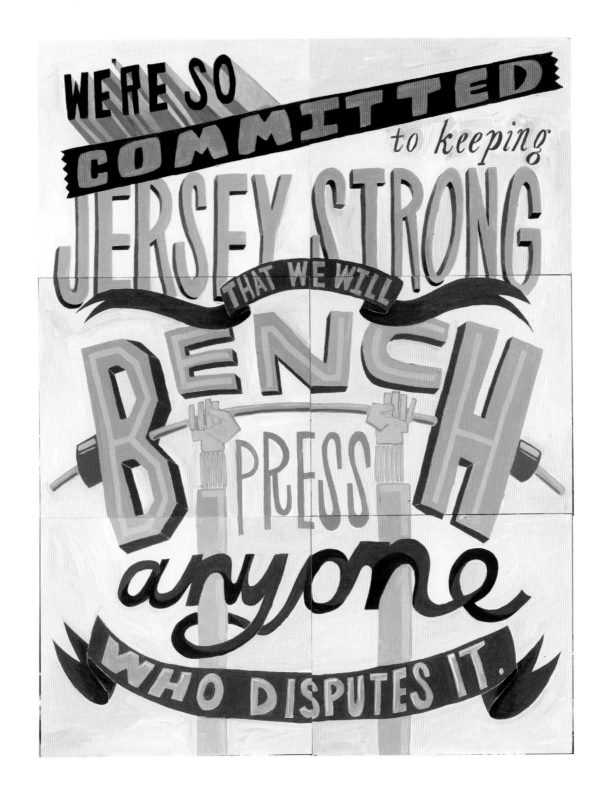

TITLE: *Freak Show*

DESIGNER: Jennifer Hammontree-Jones

"Music envelopes me and I love navigating my way through the layers to hear the messages and find personal meaning," note Jennifer Hammontree-Jones. Coming from a graphic design background, it's hard for her to separate lyrics (text) from the scenes she creates when listening to songs—and this is a lyrical piece. She says she plays in the space between sight and sound. She called her early work Album Art and kept the dimensions to 12 x 12 inches (30.5 x 30.5 cm), the same size as old LPs. With time, the 12 x 12-inch (30.5 x 30.5 cm) page size felt pretty restrained and so she went bigger and created the concept for the Concert Canvas. The one here is inspired by the song "Squirm" by the Dave Matthews Band.

"The lyrics of the song drove my interest towards the circus—bringing religion/church under the big top—and into a 'performance' venue," says says. "I think the song has much to do with comparing the two against one another and begs the question if they are so much different from one another." She researched old circus prints and canvases, notably from the Freak Shows. "I also collected related type faces and stock art images to use as reference. My use of type, perspective and color is how I maintain my style across works of art. Building messages inside messages is also something that comes through my pieces, even at times to my own surprise once I've finished a piece."

Design illuminated typographic compositions that are simultaneously almost unreadable and ornate, yet entirely legible.

STYLES: **VICTORIAN, ORNAMENTAL**

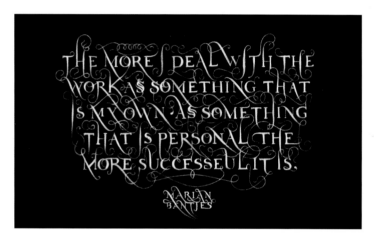

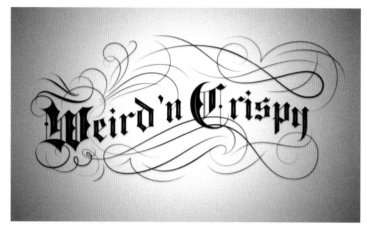

EXERCISE STEPS:

1. Brush up on ornamental lettering and handwriting from the late nineteenth century.

2. Write a headline, phrase, or paragraph that you want to illuminate.

3. Compose the layout in pencil, making certain the words are clear.

4. Overlay the ornamentation, yet make it a seamless part of the lettering.

5. Finish either by hand or computer.

6. Print out in various color combinations to determine the most legible.

TITLE: Typographic Compositions
DESIGNER: Simone Noronha

Simone Noronha is attracted to delicate, ornate, and visually complex designs. "I like getting lost in the details, and working on pieces like this is a form of meditation," she says. "I chose to imitate Marian Bantjes's style as it fit what she said so perfectly. Her work is an intense labor of love that could not be justified with a simple execution." The ornate poster is for The House Theatre of Chicago's best show at the Palmer House Hilton Hotel. This setting called for a style that matched its ornate and classic facade. The last was the start of a pet project of frequently used phrases.

PLAYFUL TIP:

Ornate lettering has become very popular. Review the current practitioners' work and then attempt to do something that blends historical and contemporary elements.

....

№45

Make a facsimile of vintage New York tabloid newspapers.

STYLES: **TABLOID, VERNACULAR**

EXERCISE STEPS:

1. Old newspapers are good foils for contemporary designs. Locate old newspaper headline typefaces from books showing vintage front pages, wood type specimen collections, or old newspapers at flea markets.

2. Find equivalent contemporary typefaces on the Web or make your own typeface.

3. Write a headline.

4. Design it to look exactly like the original but with your own content.

TITLE: *The New York Idea*
DESIGNERS: RED/Stuart Rogers and Sam Eckersley

To set the stage for an off-Broadway play about the sensationalist press, RED used the familiar language of tabloid scandal sheets. "Before divorce, scandal, and debauchery became social norms, there was *The New York Idea,*" Sam Eckersley explains. This off-Broadway play focuses on a group of turn-of-the-twentieth-century socialites who were among the first to make the news for their unseemly behavior. "The theater company asked us to steer away from an overly old-fashioned aesthetic, so we decided to base the style on current day tabloids—the really juicy ones we're all guilty of reading at the checkout line. That gave us more than enough ammo to work with. We came across a wonderful vintage image and surrounded it with a modern, dynamic type treatment, poppy colors, and a collection of enticing cover lines."

DEFINITIONS:

Parody: *an imitative work created to mock or trivialize an original work*

....

Satire: *the use of irony, sarcasm, ridicule to expose folly*

....

Pastiche: *a work that imitates the style or character of original work (though not mockingly)*

....

Facsimile: *an exact copy of written or printed material*

THE NEW YORK

IDEA

FREEWHEELING DIVORCEE READY TO SETTLE DOWN

HER EX DISAGREES!

MAN LOSES LOVE AND MONEY TO THE HORSES.

SHOCK STORY...

Lobster & Champagne on Tuesday

ADAPTED BY

DAVID AUBURN

FROM THE ORIGINAL PLAY BY

LANGDON MITCHELL

THE NEW YORK IDEA

№46

Design typography that represents, symbolizes, or illustrates an individual's personality. (It can be a friend or well-known person.)

STYLES: **ORNAMENTAL, VICTORIAN**

EXERCISE STEPS:

1. Choose someone to make into a typographic portrait. (You are not going to render the physiognomic traits of this person.)

2. Determine what style or styles best characterize this person's character.

3. Design or select characters that fit this stylistic direction.

4. Use the letterforms in any manner that best illustrates this person.

5. Print and give to the person to observe if you have touched a chord.

TITLE: *Matteo Bologna*
DESIGNER: Samia Kallidis

This typographic poster was developed for the School of Visual Arts MFA Design/Designer as Author + Entrepreneur program to promote a studio visit to Mucca Design in New York City. "Matteo Bologna's fun and lively personality called for a bright poster," explains Samia Kallidis, "with subtle references to his infamous mustache through a custom, embellished typeface and letterforms." Inspired by Mucca's work, which itself relies on historical reference," the poster is purely typographic, with a freshand lighthearted graphic language.

NOTE:

Most typographic portraits involve making faces out of typefaces. Do not resort to this common visual pun. Rather, find a more subtle way of finding the relationships.

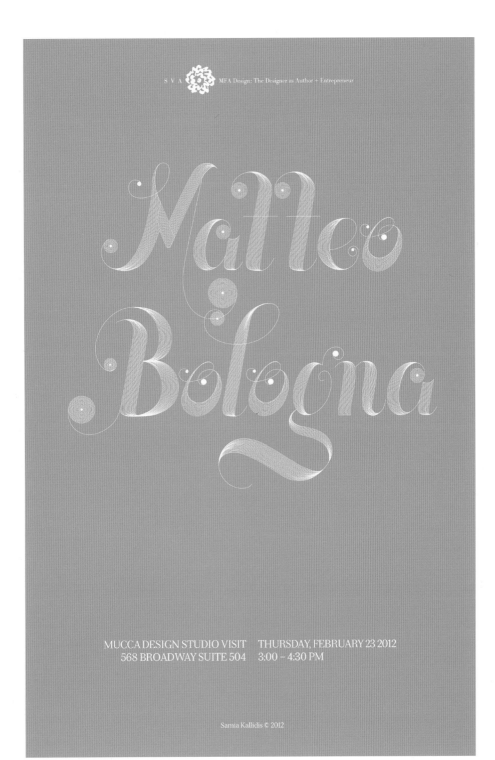

Create a series of designs in various historical styles.

STYLES: **ARTS AND CRAFTS, MODERNISTIC, CUBISM, TATTOO**

EXERCISE STEPS:

1. Research the special and distinct characteristics of each style you want to use and then sketch your interpretation using a specific theme that will carry through all your designs.

2. Draw the type by hand and incorporate it with the image to mimic the style you're after.

3. Choose colors and images that enhance the distinct qualities of the style you're communicating.

TITLE: *Viva Lewes*
DESIGNER: Neil Gower

Viva Lewes is a monthly entertainment magazine focusing on the city of Lewes in Sussex, England. Every cover must be part of a total identity integrating image and type. Neil Gower often pays homage to Matisse, Miro, and Picasso, who he copies in paintings and drawings. With every stylistic appropriation, he's teaching himself the history of art and design, if only as a "happy by-product of the process rather than what drives it," he says. "What motivates me is the desire to keep getting the thrill I first got as a kid when something alchemic happened as I was making marks on paper." Beyond that, he adds, the judicious choice of a style, or a combination of styles, can provide an additional visual cue for the viewer.

Using gauche, the cover of Viva Lewes *No. 59 suggests the racing and tourism posters of 1940s /1950s England.*

PLAYFUL TIP:

Here is an opportunity to experiment and invent your own style. Combine three existing stylistic methods together.

1. Select the styles that work best together.

2. Make a collage of all the elements to determine if they are harmonious or not.

3. Draw type or letters in those styles.

4. Make some letters ornate and others spare.

5. Combine with different subject matter to see how your new style works.

6. Put all your pieces side by side and ask your friends if they can identify each style you portrayed.

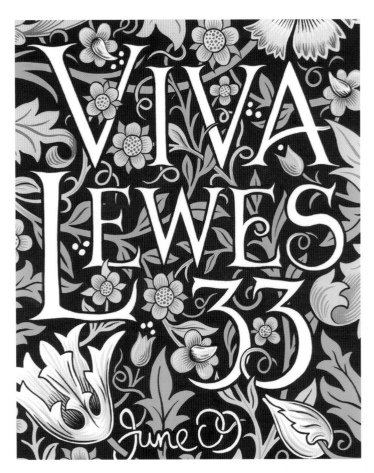

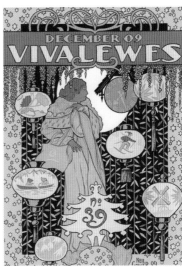

THIS PAGE

TOP LEFT:
Done in gouache, Viva Lewes, *No. 21, echoes a Miro peace poster.*

TOP RIGHT:
No. 18 harkens back to old 1930s book cover design.

BOTTOM LEFT:
No. 26 reflects an art brut approach.

BOTTOM MIDDLE AND RIGHT:
Nos. 22 and 40 have a Matisse connection.

OPPOSITE
LEFT:
No. 29 recalls the posters of James McMullan.

RIGHT TOP:
No. 35 suggests early David Hockney.

RIGHT BOTTOM:
No. 51 is contemporary storybook.

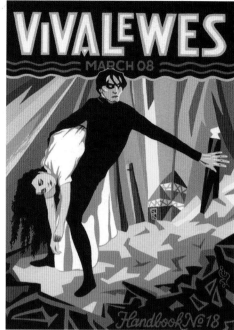

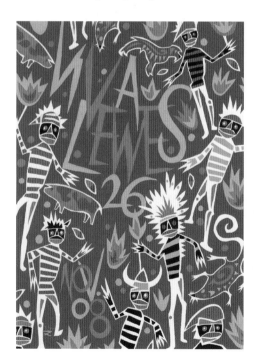

48

Make a series of silk-screen gig posters incorporating various vernacular styles, each with its own distinct character, but also with your own personal style.

STYLES: **FIFTIES VERNACULAR, PULP, COMICS, SCI-FI MODERN**

EXERCISE STEPS:

1. Starting with a blank sheet, draw the name of your favorite bands.

2. Create graphic images that represent the band's names, album title, concert theme, or style of music.

3. Limit hues, shades, and combinations to two colors.

4. Print the finish as silk screen.

TITLES: *Foo Fighters; The Gaslight Anthem; Man or Astro-Man?*

DESIGNER: Jeff Everett

The concept for this poster came from the song "Ballad of the Beaconsfield Miners" about the Baconsfield Mine collapse in Australia where the trapped miners requested an iPod with Foo Fighters' music while waiting to be freed. "The design is an attempt to create a play at a regal-looking stamp that works off a blue color background with a nod to the old, coal mining profession," says Jeff Everett. "Coal mining reminds me of blue-collar towns with long history, and I wanted to reflect that in the style of design—the lithograph/woodcut style crosshatching, the old wood type, etc."

Brian Fallon of The Gaslight Anthem loves the 1950s old Blue Note jazz albums, the cars, clothes, and the innocence that people seemed to have back then. He writes songs about love and loss, listening to music while driving your car at night near the ocean, and life on the road with your band. "I wanted to show the hard living style of being a working musician," says Jeff Everett. "It is not unlike being a sailor—every day a new town, every night a new adventure. How better to combine all these ideas than doing the poster to look like a vintage pulp novel—the kind sold behind the counter filled with wild tales of women, cars, and fisticuffs!"

This band has a long history of design featuring old sci-fi design and paintings mostly of the pulp genre. "I wanted to try something different," Jeff Everett explains. "Go vintage in feel but a more sophisticated and abstract variety. Instead of going pulpy and kitsch, I strived to make something that would belong in a '60s manual for spacemen or would look like an advertisement for the Kubrick moon landing film [*2001*]."

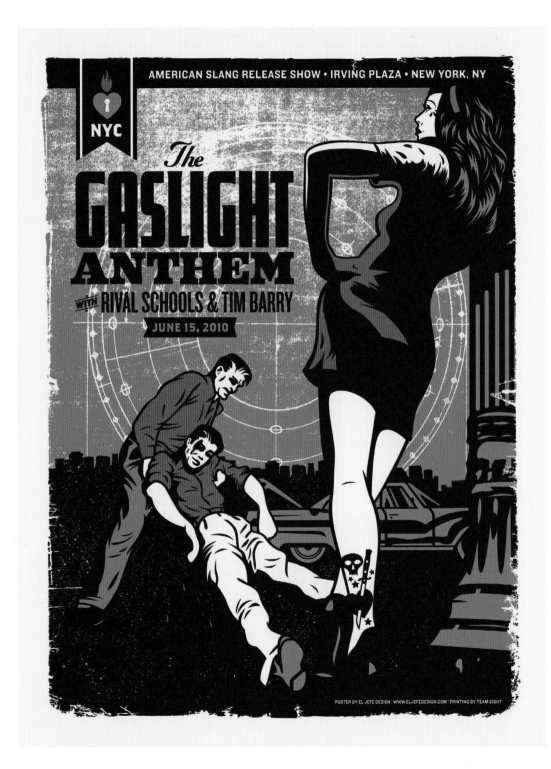

49

Design a stylized comics poster that is dense with different layers and characters, yet perfectly readable.

STYLES: **ART DECO, COMICS, ATOM**

EXERCISE STEPS:

1. Determine a theme (the inside of a ship or the workings of the human body, etc.) that is part diagram, part comic.

2. Sketch variations of the image content.

3. Compose in such a way that lettering will fit harmoniously within the image.

4. Sketch variations on the lettering.

5. Do a pencil composition. Then do a line finish.

6. Add color.

TITLE: *Nobrow*
DESIGNER: Jan Van Der Veken

London-based Nobrow publishers wanted a look inside its company building. "As a Belgian illustrator," says Jan Van Der Vekin, "I fit right in the clear line and atom style tradition of Joost Swarte and Ever Meulen, although I give a younger, more modern twist to this style. My influences in design, fashion, and architecture go back to the '30s, but my characters all have laptops and modern communication. I'm no stranger to comics, of course, and Hergé and Edgar P. Jacobs are great influences. I use a lot of the visual grammar of comics."

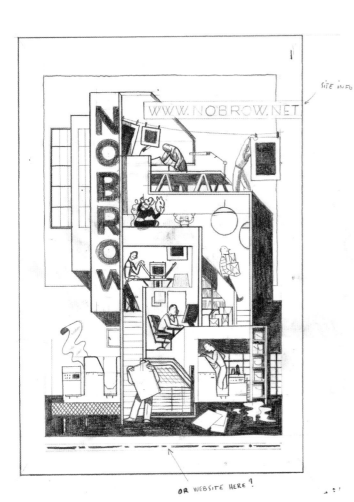

PLAYFUL TIP:

Outline drawings without shading are often the best renderings for posters.

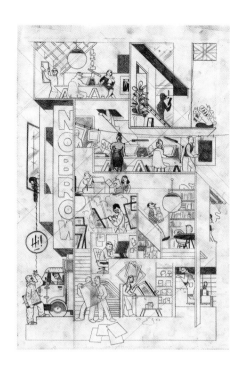

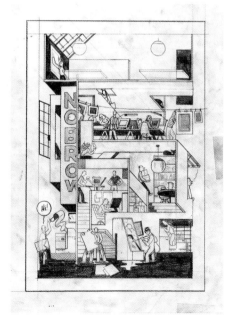

NOBROW LTD 62 GREAT EASTERN STREET LONDON EC2A 3QR INFO@NOBROW.NET

№**50**

Use any small everyday thing (paper or object) to make
a poster with a message where the "thing" that you select
is conceptually appropriate.

STYLE: **VERNACULAR**

EXERCISE STEPS:

1. Decide upon an idea and write a headline or title.

2. Choose an object (anything you want) that will be
   transformed in some way to have a double meaning.

3. Design a poster in which the object(s) are seamlessly
   integrated with the other elements (i.e., typography
   or image).

4. Photograph the composition so it appears dimensional.

TITLE: *Design, Money, and . . .*
DESIGNER: Mirko Ilić

For an AIGA lecture, Mirko Ilić chose the eternal theme of design,
money, and the big question: What else is important for a designer?
It was a perfect opportunity to design a promotional poster that
virtually answers the question. What else is important? Creative
freedom. Using common coins—pennies and dimes—to spell out the
title, Ilić reinforces the headline and provides the viewer with a simple
yet enjoyable puzzle. When seen up close, the composition is barely
readable, while at a distance the message clearly materializes—at once
clever and profound.

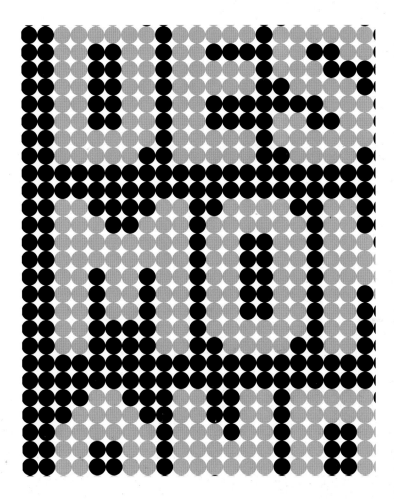

AIGA DFW Presents Mirko Ilić

May 3rd, 2010 at Clampitt Creative Center

Reception at 6:30pm followed by presentation

ACKNOWLEDGMENTS

My sincere gratitude to Emily Potts, editor, who has been a stalwart supporter of graphic design in general and my efforts in this area, specifically. It's always a joy to work with her. And to Regina Grenier, design director, with whom I have enjoyed working for many years. Thanks to Cora Hawks and Cara Connors for their production and editing work. To Rick Landers, designer, my heartfelt thanks for his talented and professional design of this and other projects. To Lita Talarico, co-chair SVA MFA Design: Designer as Author + Entrepreneur for helping to produce many talented designers. To Louise Fili, my wife, and the most brilliant typographer I know; Nick Heller, my son, a great documentary filmmaker. And, of course, thanks to all the designers who have contributed their work to this project. There would be no book without your support. —SH